JOSHUA
Bible Study
✝

ISBN: 978-0-578-87805-8

Cover and layout design by Nelly Murariu at PixBeeDesign.com.

JOSHUA
Bible Study

✝

Leading Your Family to Victorious Living One Day at a Time

Anne Gurley

I dedicate this book to my family:

Jamie Gurley, my beloved husband;

Austin, our son;

and

Elizabeth, our daughter.

Without these three people in my life,

this book would never have been written.

Table of Contents

Introduction

Victorious living is absolutely necessary for individuals and families to survive in today's world. Victory is a result of consistent, strategized steps. This one-day-at-a-time Bible study on the book of Joshua will move you and your family strategically from managing life to conquering life.

Joshua was a man who was mightily used by God to lead his family and the nation of Israel into the Promised Land. He remained faithful to God and the people he led for many years and through numerous life experiences.

In this day-by-day walk through the book of Joshua, you and your family will relive the victories and setbacks Joshua experienced. You will learn how to live victoriously today in your current circumstances. You will learn strategies to use against the enemies in your life. You will learn to depend on God who fights for you and leads the way to your victory.

Included in this study are *Interesting Facts*, *Parent Encouragement*, *Family Projects*, *Bible Memorization Challenges*, and much more. These resources will encourage your family to spend time together and walk together on this journey of victory. Through this study, you'll have the opportunity to implement the strategies necessary to win.

This book is designed to boost your family from mundane living to triumphant living through the study and application of God's Word.

Let's begin; victory is just a day away!

ABC's to Most Effectively Use This Book

A. **Acclimate** yourself to the resources scattered throughout the book. Your family may benefit if you took a few minutes to pre-plan before each gathering. However, pre-planning is not required.

B. **Believe** the seeds you sow will be used by God to your family's benefit.

C. **Change.** Study with no change is of no benefit. Use the *Thoughts and Observations for Victorious Living* section at the end of each day to strategize how your family could do things differently, how you could draw different conclusions about God or yourself, and how you could determine to live victoriously based on these thoughts and observations.

D. **Do it!** Just do it. Even if you don't feel like it or think you don't have time. Cheer one another on to victory.

E. **Engage** your whole family together to think spiritually for victorious daily living. Take advantage of the sections titled, *A Word About* after each fifth day for unique topical discussions. Expand your understanding with the *More Facts* section at the back.

F. **Fun.** Have fun. There are many *Family Project Ideas* that are included to encourage family fun. These are moments that will provide hands-on teachable opportunities.

G. **Give** your all. You will see in this study that Joshua, as the leader, gave his all. Your family follows your example. Give your all and you will encourage your family to give their all.

H.   Help one another. This is not a competition. You may know all the answers, or you may not know any of the answers. Work together to locate the answers and apply what your family learns.

I.   Include others. Your children may have friends visit who can be included in this study. You may never know the impact you will make on someone else by including them in a *Bible Memorization Challenge* or a *Find It* activity.

J.   Journey. The process of learning is a journey. Think of this as a journey, not a sprint. Though this study is set up in 50 days and should be able to be done in 10 weeks, your family may choose to take as long as a year to complete it and establish one night a week as "The Joshua Journey Night." Do not be in a hurry. Enjoy the journey. Learn from the journey. Take as little or as much time as necessary to achieve the victorious result.

K.   Keep your date. Schedule the *Joshua Bible Study* as an event on your family calendar. When another event arises for the time/date you have set for your family gathering, say "We're booked for that time. We won't be able to make it."

L.   Love the Lord your God. Demonstrate your love for God and love for your family as you involve them in studying God's Word, learning strategies for knowing how to please God, and experiencing victorious living.

M. Memorize Bible passages together. Make it a true challenge. Include competitions with prizes. Use in-person or video opportunities to promote your child's public speaking abilities with family and friends using the *Bible Memorization Challenges*.

N.   No one left out. Though this study is primarily for families with children ages 8 to 12, no one in your family should be left out. There are many ways the *Joshua Bible Study* can be adapted for younger family members or older family members. If you have an adult relative visiting at a time you're doing the *Joshua Bible Study*, have them join in. They may have expertise to share you didn't know about.

O. Obsess over nothing. There are multiple *Interesting Facts* and *Parent Encouragement* sections scattered throughout the study. Do not obsess over reading every one of them. They were included to support and encourage your road to victorious living. If time is an issue, skip these parts.

P. Pray always. Be sure to include an exchange with God about your family's involvement in this study privately and in the company of your family. At the end of your gathering, pray about what you've learned. Ask God to write the words of His Word and the concepts learned on the heart of each member of your family, starting with yours.

Q. Quick to hear. Teach your children to be quick to hear the Word of God. Encourage them to understand that the Word of God is the most valuable thing they could ever possess in life, so they need to be quiet and quick to hear.

R. Respond. Respond to your family's questions about what they are learning. Teach your children to respond to God's Word. There are a multitude of opportunities to discuss various passages of Scripture. These were included to encourage your family to process God's Word for the purpose of applying it to daily living. This process of engagement will encourage a proper response to God's Word.

S. Setting is key to learning. Get rid of distractions. Gather in a place that is comfortable for reading, learning, and communicating.

T. Time it right. Set the timer if needed for the time allotment established. When the time is up, wrap up the session. This will encourage efficient use of time. It will avoid boredom and loss of interest. It is recommended to spend 15 to 20 minutes on each day. More time can be spent, however twenty minutes may be plenty for your family. If you want to utilize more of the resources available, you may choose to take more than one gathering to complete a day.

U. Utilize other resources. The Internet has a large number of resources and maps that would be helpful in viewing the cities and territories discussed in the Joshua Bible Study. Get your family involved. Assign them "research projects" to find maps for the gatherings.

V. Voice the Scriptures. There are many, many difficult words in this study. Do not allow yourself or your family to be intimidated by not knowing how to pronounce these words. Use an online resource like Bible Gateway (biblegateway.com) to listen to the daily text. Use your own voices to read and hear the text. Always read the text for the day before beginning to answer the questions.

W. Write it down. At the beginning of each section, there is space for observations and questions to be recorded. As the Scripture is being read or after it is read, take time to write down anything that comes to mind about the Scripture. This will encourage independent thinking. Then write the answers to the questions provided.

X. X-ray vision. Look into your inner man as you study the passages. Encourage your family to search inside themselves to ensure alignment from the heart to the Word of God.

Y. YouTube It! Video your family gatherings, *Family Project Ideas*, *Bible Memorization Challenge* matches, etc. Share the videos with family and friends.

Z. Zeal. Be full of zeal as you are intentional to lead your family to victory. Your journey will not look like that of another family. Your family is unique. Your journey of learning will be unique. Be zealous and always abounding in your family's victorious living.

Keep track of your *One Day at a Time Victorious Living* here.

1 ☐	2 ☐	3 ☐	4 ☐	5 ☐
6 ☐	7 ☐	8 ☐	9 ☐	10 ☐
11 ☐	12 ☐	13 ☐	14 ☐	15 ☐
16 ☐	17 ☐	18 ☐	19 ☐	20 ☐
21 ☐	22 ☐	23 ☐	24 ☐	25 ☐
26 ☐	27 ☐	28 ☐	29 ☐	30 ☐
31 ☐	32 ☐	33 ☐	34 ☐	35 ☐
36 ☐	37 ☐	38 ☐	39 ☐	40 ☐
41 ☐	42 ☐	43 ☐	44 ☐	45 ☐
46 ☐	47 ☐	48 ☐	49 ☐	50 ☐

Dear Parents,

Establishing a consistent habit of
Bible reading and Bible study will
enable your child to have good success.

<table>
<tr><td></td><td># The Backstory Exposed</td></tr>
</table>

Who is the book of Joshua about, and who wrote it?

Joshua was a man who lived in Egypt before the Exodus. The events around the Exodus are recorded in the book of Exodus in the Old Testament. Joshua had firsthand knowledge of God's authority in delivering the children of Israel out of Egypt, God's power in the crossing of the Red Sea, God's provision in the wilderness, and many other mighty acts God performed for His people. Joshua believed God would allow them to win over the giants and enter in the land God had promised. Ten other men who spied the land with Joshua failed to believe God's promise. These ten men died in the wilderness because of their unbelief. Joshua had believed God despite the opinions of others. Joshua's consistent habit of trusting God gave him opportunity to enter the Promised Land and lead others in as well. Joshua focused on God's ability and did not neglect allegiance to Him even when the majority failed to enter the provision of God because of unbelief.

The name Joshua means "savior," or "whose help is Jehovah." Joshua was 40 years old when he left Egypt. He was 80 at the beginning of the book of Joshua.

Joshua is believed to be the author of the book of Joshua. However, today there are supposed scholars who dispute the authorship of Joshua. They say the book was written much later. However, the earliest records are usually most accurate. Therefore, except for the last few verses which record Joshua's death, it is believed Joshua wrote the book of Joshua.

When was Joshua written?

The book of Joshua was written around 1400 B.C.

What is Joshua about?

Joshua is a historical book of the Bible. It records God calling Joshua to take Moses' place and lead the children of Israel into the Promised Land. The Promised Land was the land God had promised to give His people. The book records the battles fought to conquer the land. The dividing of the Promised Land was recorded in Joshua. The book concludes with Joshua addressing the people and encouraging the people to continually follow God, as well as the events surrounding his death.

What Can We Look Forward to Learning from Joshua?

- † God is faithful to keep His promises.
- † God acts powerfully on behalf of His people.
- † God requests and deserves whole-hearted obedience.

What is One Key Verse from Joshua?

Joshua 1:8-9, KJV: *"This Book of the Law shall not depart from your mouth, but you shall meditate on it day and night, so that you may be careful to do according to all that is written in it. For then you will make your way prosperous, and then you will have good success. Have I not commanded you? Be strong and courageous. Do not be frightened, and do not be dismayed, for the Lord your God is with you wherever you go."*

Why Should We Study the Book of Joshua?

2 Timothy 3:16-17, ESV: *"All Scripture is breathed out by God and profitable for teaching, for reproof, for correction, and for train-ing in righteousness, that the man of God may be complete, equipped for every good work."*

✏️ **Thoughts and Observations for Victorious Living**

   † Who wrote the book of Joshua? _____

   † Joshua was written (before/after) Jesus died.

   † What does the name Joshua mean? _____

   † Look up and read Deuteronomy 31:7-8. Joshua knew about
     God because he listened when Moses spoke about God.
     How do you think you can know more about God?

_____

_____

_____

_____

_____

_____

_____

_____

Dear Parents,

You never get too old for God to remind you
of His faithfulness to fulfill His promise.

Joshua's Mission

Read Joshua 1:1-9

✎ Observations & Questions You Have from the Passage

_____

_____

_____

_____

_____

_____

Knowing for Yourself

Who died? _____

Who spoke to Joshua? _____

Joshua was known as a person who (helped/fought against) Moses.

...

Order the events God told Joshua to do after Moses died. Label the events 1 to 4.

- ☐ Go over the Jordan.

- ☐ Take the people with you.

- ☐ Go into the land I give to the children of Israel.

- ☐ Arise.

God would give (all/some) of the land they walked on.

God promised He would be with Joshua as He had been with

_____ .

God promised to never fail or forsake Joshua. What does that mean about God? _____

_____

_____

God told Joshua in verses 6, 7, and 9 to be "strong and very courageous." Think about the reasons God told Joshua he needed to be strong and very courageous:

- † Joshua would give the land to the people that God had promised.
- † Joshua would do everything written in God's Word as given by Moses.
- † Joshua would not be afraid or dismayed.

...

When God tells us to be "strong and very courageous," there is usually a promise of provision associated. What were the promises associated with each of these ways for Joshua to be strong?

The people would get _____ .

Joshua would prosper and have _____ .

God would be with _____ wherever he went.

...

Verses 8 and 9 explain what Joshua should do with The Book of the Law. What were Joshua's instructions?

- † Be careful to do all that it says.
- † Think about it day and night.

...

What was the promise of God when Joshua was careful to do and think about all God said in The Book of the Law? _____

_____

_____

_____

_____

_____

 Thoughts and Observations for Victorious Living

- † God is faithful. He keeps His Word.

- † Our ability to be strong and of great courage is directly related to our trust God will be with us and help us.

- † God gives us an ability to be strong and of great courage so that we may be careful to know, to think about, and to do all God has instructed.

- † Prosperity and success that are worth having are because we have obeyed and God has provided.

> **ⓘ INTERESTING FACT**
>
> As New Testament believers, we can take courage using 2 Timothy 1:7.
>
> God has given us a spirit of ability to do what He's told us to do.

Dear Parents,

Your duty as a parent is to help your children.
Always go ahead of them with all your might
to help them enter the rest of God.

| Day Three | **The People Get Ready**
Read Joshua 1:10-18 |

✒ Observations & Questions You Have from the Passage

_____

_____

_____

_____

_____

_____

Knowing for Yourself

Joshua commanded the officers and the officers told the
_____ to get ready.

The message was for the people to prepare provision because in
_____ days they would be going over the Jordan to possess
the land.

Who was giving the people the land? _____

What type of body of water was the Jordan? _____

_____

INTERESTING FACT

The Jordan was the "chief watering place." In the Gospel of John, it was the place where John the Baptist baptized. Jesus was baptized in the Jordan River.

 FIND IT: At the beginning of Joshua, the people are in the Plains of Moab. Locate a map of the Plains of Moab and the Jordan River.

There were 12 tribes of the children of Israel. The tribes were named for the children of Jacob, who was also called by the name of Israel. Jacob was Abraham's grandson. The book of Genesis tells the story of Abraham, Isaac (Jacob's father), and Jacob. Jacob's family moved to Egypt. When they arrived in Egypt, there were only seventy people in the family. While they lived in Egypt, their population grew to be about a million people.

The children of Israel were identified according to tribes. The tribes were named Reuben, Simeon, Levi (the priestly tribe), Judah, Zebulun, Issachar, Dan, Gad, Asher, Naphtali, Joseph (often listed as two tribes named for his sons, Ephraim and Manasseh), and Benjamin. These were the names of Jacob's sons. (Notice Reuben, Gad, and part of Manasseh were on the right of the Jordan River.)

Before the book of Joshua begins, Moses had given Reuben, Gad, and part of Manasseh the land on the east side of the Jordan. The people requested Moses to let them settle there because they had a lot of animals and did not want to take them across the

Family Project Idea

Make a family tree starting with Abraham and ending with the children of Jacob.

Jordan River. Joshua requested all the armed men of the tribes of Reuben, Gad, and Manasseh that had settled on the east of the Jordan to help the other tribes conquer the land.

How did the people respond to Joshua's request to go conquer the land? Also include who the people wanted Joshua to have with him and what would happen to the person who did not obey Joshua.

_____

_____

_____

 Thoughts and Observations for Victorious Living

† Leaders (including parents) should always get their direction from the Lord.

† Christians should help other believers fight to find rest even if they've already found it.

† The most important thing is to be strong in the Lord (knowledge of Him and His Word) and very courageous (take a stand for what God says to do and do it).

FOR DISCUSSION

How important was it for the people to follow Joshua? Did the people take it seriously? How serious are you to follow your leaders?

Dear Parents,

Rahab kept the men of the One True God close to her. She sent the men seeking to set themselves over the One True God on a chase into nothingness. Encourage your children to always keep the One True God close and direct any who seek to dethrone the One True God far away.

	# God Always Protects Read Joshua 2:1-7

✎ Observations & Questions You Have from the Passage

_____

_____

_____

_____

_____

_____

_____

Knowing for Yourself

Who sent out the spies?

_____

How many spies were there?

_____

The spies were supposed to go view the land all the way to _____ .

When they came to Jericho, to whose house did they go?

_____

> 📍 **FIND IT:**
> **On a map, locate the following:**
> † The Plains of Moab
> † The Jordan River
> † The Ford of Jordan
> † Jericho

What was Rahab's occupation? _____

Who heard the spies were in Jericho? _____

What did Rahab do with the spies? _____

_____

 INTERESTING FACT

Rahab hid the spies among the stalks of flax.
Flax was used to make linen cloth. The flax has
stems that can cause decay in the material if not
removed. The removal process was to allow the
cut stalks to stay in the dew until the stem that
contained the toxin separated from the plant.
Then the stem could be removed and the flax
used to make clothes that would not decay.
Rahab probably had stalks of flax on her roof
because she was in the process of making clothes.

Did the king's men find the spies? _____

What did Rahab tell the king's men about the spies? (Check all that
apply.)

☐ "Some men came to my house."
☐ "I didn't know where the men were from."
☐ "I hid the spies on the roof."
☐ "The spies went out of the gate. Go look for them."

...

After the king's men went out of the gate, the gate was

_____ .

How far did the king's men go to pursue the spies? _____

✏ Thoughts and Observations for Victorious Living

† God provides protection for His people.

† God allows escape from danger for His people.

INTERESTING FACT

A ford is a shallow place with good footing where a river or stream may be crossed by wading, or inside a vehicle getting its wheels wet. A ford is mostly a natural phenomenon, in contrast to a low water crossing, which is an artificial bridge that allows crossing a river or stream when water is low.

FOR DISCUSSION

Discuss Psalm 51:6 – Rahab lied to the king's messengers. Did she obey God when she lied? God desires truth in the inward heart of a person. What are your thoughts about God using a lying harlot to protect His people?

Dear Parents,

Be willing to put yourself at risk by telling of your need and the need of your family. Be concerned enough about your family's well-being to ask for help.

Day Five

The Enemy is Faint

Read Joshua 2:8-24

✎ Observations & Questions You Have from the Passage

_____

_____

_____

_____

_____

_____

Knowing for Yourself

What did Rahab tell the men? (Check all that apply.)

Quote of Hope

Our past victories should encourage us in defeat of our current enemies.

☐ God would give the children of Israel the land where she lived.

☐ When the children of Israel left Egypt, the people of Jericho heard how God had parted the Red Sea and allowed the people to pass over on dry ground.

☐ The Amorite kings had won when the children of Israel fought against them.

☐ The Lord of the children of Israel is God of heaven and earth.

What did Rahab want the men to do? (Check all that apply.)

☐ Give her some food.

☐ Save her and her family.

☐ Repay her for her kindness to them.

...

What did the spies agree to do? (Check all that apply.)

☐ If Rahab were to tell others about the spies, her household would be saved.

☐ If Rahab were to tell others about the spies, her household would not be saved.

☐ Rahab would have to get everyone who wanted to be saved into her house.

...

Where was Rahab's house located in the city? _____

How did she help the spies get out of the city? _____

_____

She told the spies to go to the _____ and stay there for _____ days.

Rahab was to put a _____ cord/rope in the window so the spies would know where her house was when they returned.

Where was Rahab's family supposed to stay until the men came back to destroy Jericho? _____

If anybody who was in the house was killed, who would be guilty?

_____

...

If anybody was killed who was not in the house, who would be guilty?

_____

The men went back to _____ after they had stayed

_____ in the mountains.

...

What did the men report when they returned to their people? (Check all that apply.)

☐ The people are scared of us.

☐ We met a really pretty lady named Rahab.

☐ There were men chasing us and they found us.

☐ God is going to let us take possession of Jericho.

✐ Thoughts and Observations for Victorious Living

†   God desires men everywhere to fear and revere Him.

†   God uses men and women to help perform His work on earth.

†   God is the God of heaven and earth.

INTERESTING FACT

Rahab made the scarlet cord so everyone could see it but not everyone understood the meaning, Jesus taught in parables. Though everyone heard the story, not everyone understood the meaning.

(Matthew 13:13)

A WORD ABOUT PRAYER

Rahab *prayed* to the spies. She was asking them to spare her life and her family. She knew she was in danger and asked the spies for help because she knew they were her only hope of survival. She demonstrated an allegiance to the spies by hiding them from the officials. This kindness to the strangers was an active way to plead with them for mercy. She wanted the spies to spare her own life and the life of her family. Everyone who came into her house, she wanted to be spared from destruction. She hid the spies to "buy more time" to plead for her life and the life of her family.

Prayer is recognizing we need help and calling on the only one who can help. In the New Testament, Jesus told a parable of a widow. He told this story to teach us to pray and not to give up. Jesus wanted to show the importance of always praying. The widow's story is found in Luke 18:1-8. She continually went to the town's judge day after day, beating on his door, and asking for protection from her enemy. Because the judge was weary with her continual coming, he gave her what she asked. Jesus concluded the parable by saying that God is much kinder than the "unjust judge" in the story. Therefore, God would hear and answer those who ask Him for help.

Rahab had never heard the story of the unjust judge, but she lingered with the spies and continued to ask them for deliverance from destruction. She knew God would be destroying the city she lived in. She asked the only people who could do anything about it.

When you pray, pray to God. Pray to the only One who can do something about your situation. Sometimes when we pray, we do not know the outcome. We do not know how it will turn out. But pray to God always, don't give up, and diligently ask for help from the only One who can do anything about your situation. (See Matthew 7:7-8 for more encouragement.)

NOTES

_____

_____

_____

_____

_____

_____

_____

_____

_____

_____

_____

_____

_____

_____

_____

_____

_____

Dear Parents,

Remember to give your children specific things to look for in life and teach them how to respond when those things are visible.

<table>
<tr><td>

Day Six

</td><td>

All the People Cross Over the Jordan

Read Joshua 3:1-17

</td></tr>
</table>

✐ Observations & Questions You Have from the Passage

_____

_____

_____

_____

_____

_____

Knowing for Yourself

Where did Joshua arrive after he left Shittim? _____

How long did they stay in this new place? _____

What were the people told to look for before they should move again? _____

How much space was to be between the people? _____

Why did they have to keep such a great distance?

A. They couldn't get close to the priests.

B. They hadn't gone through this land before.

 INTERESTING FACT

A cubit is 18 inches and can often be measured by the distance between the elbow and the tip of the longest finger when held out.

Because of the great things they were expecting, the people were to sanctify themselves. What does that mean?

_____

_____

Sanctification Explored

For God "to do wonders among us," we must set ourselves apart by being holy, separate, pure, and distinct. This is what it means to be sanctified. Joshua instructed the people they must be focused on God. In our day, God tells us our focus should be on Him also. We should be pure, distinct, and separated unto God. (1 Thessalonians 4:3)

God being with us is what drives out corruption and enables us to have an abundant life. (John 10:10) In addition, we can be encouraged in the truth of Philippians 4:13, NIV – "I can do all things through him who strengthens me." When we are separated unto God, He is with us, and God makes the way to victory even when it seems impossible.

God told Joshua He would make all the people (hate/respect) him just like they had done to Moses. God wanted the people to know He was with Joshua and helping him lead the people.

Joshua told the people the following: (Check all that apply.)

☐ "The Lord wanted me to tell you something."

☐ "The Lord is with us."

☐ "The Lord will not allow you to win over the people of the land."

☐ "Take eight men of the tribes and have them get stones."

Family Project Idea

Determine how much distance 2,000 cubits would measure. Measure the distance off. Recreate the scene as stated in Joshua 3.

What did the priests carry? _____

What happened when the priests stepped into the water?

_____

Did all the people pass over on dry ground? _____

✎ Thoughts and Observations for Victorious Living

✝   God guides us by His Word to go through places we have never been before.

✝   God assures us through our leaders and our circumstances that He is with us and will not fail us.

✝   God expects us to do what He directs. That is how we have success.

📍 **FIND IT:** Locate a picture online of the Ark of the Covenant to see what it looked like.

Dear Parents,

Determine to set up family traditions. These will serve as remembrances for your children. Also, know that God will "magnify" you to your children as you lead them according to the Word of God.

Setting Up a Remembrance

Read Joshua 4:1-18

✎ Observations & Questions You Have from the Passage

_____

_____

_____

_____

_____

_____

Knowing for Yourself

When did the Lord tell Joshua to choose twelve men from among the people?

    A. Before the people started crossing over.

    B. While the people were crossing over.

    C. After the people had crossed over.

INTERESTING FACT

Jesus told us to use the Lord's Supper to remember His death for us until He comes. 1 Corinthians 11:23-26

What was each of the twelve men supposed to do? (Put the list in order 1, 2, 3, 4.)

- ☐ Pick up a stone from the dry land of the Jordan.
- ☐ Leave the stone where they would be staying the night.
- ☐ Go to the priests in the Jordan.
- ☐ Take the stone to the place where they'd stay.

How were the men supposed to carry the stones? _____

_____

...

What was the purpose of them getting stones from the Jordan and setting them up where they would be spending the night?

A. They needed to do something.
B. They could tell their children about God's doings in the future.

...

The priests stood in the middle of the Jordan until _____ was finished that the Lord commanded Joshua to speak unto the people.

Waiting Explored

Pay attention until everything is finished. The priests stayed in the water until all was finished. They had to be patient to ensure all the instructions were complete and everything they were to do had been done.

Jesus continued to wait, listen, and obey until the end, when on the cross He said, "IT IS FINISHED." John 19:28-30

Who made the people respect and reverence Joshua? _____

...

_____ told Joshua is was time for the priests to come out of the Jordan River.

...

What happened when the priests came out of the Jordan River?

_____

 Thoughts and Observations for Victorious Living

- † God wants us to remember the mighty acts He has done for others and for us. A visual reminder is a good way to remember the way God's power is displayed.
- † God's message is proclaimed from one generation to the next.
- † God is honored when His Word is promptly obeyed.
- † We should follow the leaders God has placed before us without grumbling and complaining.

FOR DISCUSSION

Discuss what "appoint" means. You may find a dictionary and/or thesaurus to help your discussion.

Discuss the traditions your family, and that of your ancestors, have established which proclaim God's message from one generation to the next. Are there any others you could establish?

Dear Parents,

Set up memorials and share with your
children the mighty acts of God in your life.
When your children see and hear of how
God has worked in your life, it will encourage
them to respect God and follow His ways.

The People Respect God

Read Joshua 4:19–5:12

✐ Observations & Questions You Have from the Passage

_____

_____

_____

_____

_____

_____

Knowing for Yourself

The name of the place they lived for a while after crossing over the Jordan was _____ and they arrived at this place on the _____ day of the _____ month.

They brought _____ stones and Joshua put them up in Gilgal.

The stones were put up for the _____ to ask and be told Israel came over the Jordan on dry

Family Project Idea

Begin keeping a journal of meaningful events in the life of your family.

_____

ground because God dried up the waters and the Israelites passed over.

God dried up the Jordan River like He had dried up the _____ .

Joshua told the people all the earth should know the hand of the Lord is mighty. What was the reason and what is the proper response when this is known? _____

INTERESTING FACT

The fear of the Lord is the beginning of wisdom. To fear the Lord means you honor and respect Him above all else. Proverbs 9:10

The kings of the Amorites and the Canaanites were _____ when they heard what the Lord had done and the people passed over on dry ground.

God told Joshua to circumcise the males because they had not done it while journeying through the wilderness. Was God in agreement with them not being circumcised in the wilderness?

Circumcision Explored

In the Old Testament, circumcision was an outward sign the person was a follower of God. Today, God desires the outward sign of being a follower of God to be based on the attitude and actions of our heart. God desires our will and inner man to be circumcised. The habits and practices in our life should be whole commitment to following God and His way of doing things. 1 Corinthians 7:19

After the procedures were done, the people stayed in the place until they were well. The Lord told Joshua He had rolled away the blame of Egypt. This caused the place to be named _____ (rolling). Note: The people stopped circumcising their children while in Egypt because of the bondage they were in and it was "just too difficult" to keep up the covenant of God.

Then, while in the wilderness, they chose not to keep up the covenant. Therefore, God revived the covenant and took away their blame for not keeping the covenant in Egypt and in the wilderness.

...

The children of Israel stayed at Gilgal and celebrated _____ on the fourteenth day of the first month. The manna God had provided in the wilderness was no longer provided. What did the people eat for the rest of the year? _____

_____

Thoughts and Observations for Victorious Living

† God demands complete obedience so that His name and glory are honored.

† God's provision never runs out too early. His timing is perfect.

FOR DISCUSSION

Discuss how each member of your family respects God.

Dear Parents,

Encourage your children to decide to be on God's side and be His follower. Jesus said in Matthew 12:30 and Luke 11:23, those who are not with Him are against Him. Encourage your child to be with the Lord, and not against Him. The decision should take place at the earliest point possible before the battles of life.

The Captain Gives Orders

Read Joshua 5:13-6:11

✎ **Observations & Questions You Have from the Passage**

_____

_____

_____

_____

_____

_____

Knowing for Yourself

Joshua saw a man with a drawn sword and asked him a question. What did Joshua ask the man? _____

_____

How did the man respond? _____

When Joshua found out who it was, what did Joshua do?

_____

...

The Lord told Joshua to take off his shoes, for the place he was standing was _____ .

INTERESTING FACT

It is believed this captain of the host of the Lord was actually an appearance of Jesus. When Jesus appears in the Old Testament, it is called a Christophany.

Jericho was open and everyone in the city went in and out freely. (True/False)

The Lord said He had given Jericho into the hand of Joshua (before/after) the walls fell down.

Who told Joshua to march around the city of Jericho for six days?

_____

What would happen the seventh day?

    A. They would go around the city _____ times.

    B. Seven priests would blow seven _____ .

When they blew the horns, the blast would be (short/long).

What would happen to the walls of Jericho? _____

_____

> **"A whole lot of what we call 'struggling' is simply delayed obedience."**
>
> **~ Elisabeth Elliot**

Every man would go up and capture the men that were (beside them/ in front of them).

Who/What went first, second, etc.? Put the following in order. (Label 1, 2, 3, 4)

- ☐ People

- ☐ Priests with trumpets

- ☐ Ark of the Lord

- ☐ The armed men

Could the people say anything? (Yes/No)

On the first day after they walked around the city, what did the people do? _____

...

Thoughts and Observations for Victorious Living

- † God is holy and must be respected and honored.

- † God always has a plan of action.

- † God always knows what is going to happen before it happens.

- † God expects us to do what He says, because He knows what is best for us and gives us directions that are meant to be followed.

FOR DISCUSSION

From a man's perspective, did it matter whether they made any sound, talked, or spoke while marching around the city? Why did they have to be quiet? Why do we sometimes have to do things our leaders say even when it does not seem important for it to be done that way?

Dear Parents,

Be an example for your children. Joshua rose early and the priests took up the ark of the Lord. Be sure to go before your children, leading their way, and always having the presence of the Lord with you.

The Walls of Jericho Fall Down

Read Joshua 6:12-25

✐ Observations & Questions You Have from the Passage

_____

_____

_____

_____

_____

_____

Knowing for Yourself

What did they do for six days?

_____

Were the trumpets being blown (making noise)? (Yes/No)

What time of day did their march get started on the seventh day?

_____

 FIND IT: Write a math problem that would figure how many total times the children of Israel walked around Jericho. How many times did you figure?

How many times did they march around the city on the seventh day?

_____

What was different about the seventh time around on the seventh day?

_____

What happened to the city?

_____

Every person in the city was to be destroyed except for the people in whose house?

_____

_____

Family Project Idea

Mark out a distance of about a mile. Walk that distance early in the morning for six days without making any sounds. Then on the seventh day, walk the distance seven times. Get the walk started at dawn. On the seventh time around, make lots of noise.

Why were the people in this house spared? _____

_____

...

Make a list of everything God told the people to destroy in the city:

_____   _____   _____

_____   _____   _____

_____   _____   _____

...

Who did Joshua send to get Rahab? _____

_____

What did they do to the city and everything that was there?

_____

Bible Memorization Challenge—Ephesians 2:8-9

 ## Thoughts and Observations for Victorious Living

✝ When we obey God's instructions, everything works just like He says it will work.

✝ "The wealth of the sinner is laid up for the just." ~ Matthew Henry

✝ God assures us of the outcome and success of His plan before we even begin to do what He has planned.

FOR DISCUSSION

Discuss how the favor of God (grace) was shown to Rahab and her family. Why were they spared and the rest of the city destroyed? What can we learn from the actions of Rahab and those who were with her in the house? Would you have chosen to be in the house? What is your reason?

A WORD ABOUT FAITH

Rahab's faith is the cause of her salvation. Hebrews 11:31 says she was not destroyed because she welcomed the spies *by faith*. Faith is a confidence in God. It is an assurance of what God has said He will do.

Faith comes through hearing God's Word and believing it (Romans 10:17). Forty years earlier, the children of Israel crossed over the Red Sea on dry ground. Rahab had heard how God had spared the children of Israel and drowned all the Egyptians. We are not aware of Rahab's age at the time of the Red Sea event or at the time of the Jericho event. We are only told what she did to make a living. There is no mention she had any husband or children. Her mother, father, and brothers were mentioned as being in her house and being rescued. She may have been old enough when the Red Sea event occurred to have heard the reports firsthand. However, she may have heard others tell the stories of what happened "years before." Either way, she *heard* and *believed*.

The faith of Rahab pleased God. She was confident in God for many reasons. She had not only heard of the Red Sea event, she had also heard how God had utterly destroyed several kings and their kingdoms. Because of what she had heard, she believed God was the God of heaven and earth. Hebrews 11:6 says anyone who comes to God must believe that He is God and He gives back to anyone who looks to find Him. Rahab acted *by faith* when the spies came. She knew God would destroy the city of Jericho and she wanted to be spared. She had confidence in God being the God of heaven and earth. She was assured whatever God decided would be done. She knew God rewarded and took care of those who followed Him. She had heard God destroyed those who fought against God and His people. Rahab wanted to be on God's side, not against Him.

Because of Rahab's faith, she was not destroyed. Her family and all that were in her house were saved. She had shared her faith. She had spoken of her confidence in God. She had proclaimed to those in her company, "GOD IS THE GOD OF HEAVEN AND EARTH." She had spoken many times, rehearsing God's rescue of the children of Israel and His destruction of the Egyptians. She had told how the great and mighty kings of Sihon and Og had been overthrown by a group of people fleeing Egypt. She knew only God could create these wins. She wanted to be part of the winning team.

Faith, confidence in God, made her part of the winning team. Rahab's dependence on God by faith saved her.

NOTES

_____

_____

_____

_____

_____

_____

_____

_____

Dear Parents,

Teach your children to know they can keep you from knowing their secrets, but they can never keep any secret from God.

Day Eleven	# Here Comes Trouble
	Read Joshua 6:26-7:9

✐ Observations & Questions You Have from the Passage

_____

_____

_____

_____

_____

_____

_____

Knowing for Yourself

What would happen to the person who attempted to rebuild Jericho?

_____

What was the result of God being with Joshua? What did the people think of Joshua? _____

_____

What made God burn with anger? _____

_____

Did Joshua know anyone had displeased God? _____

_____

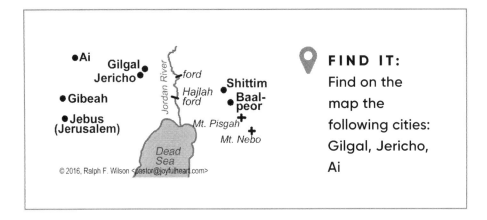

FIND IT:
Find on the map the following cities: Gilgal, Jericho, Ai

The spies came back and told Joshua which of the following:

    A. There are many people there, we need to use all the troops.

    B. There are not many people there, we don't need to use all the troops.

How many men from the children of Israel went up to Ai?

_____

Who won the battle? _____

How many people of the children of Israel died? _____

What did the people's hearts feel like? _____

What did Joshua and the elders do?

    ✝   Tore their _____ .

    ✝   Fell before _____ .

    ✝   Put _____ on their heads.

 INTERESTING FACT:

A melted heart is a way of feeling that runs all over the place. It is discouraged, lacks stability, faint, and out of control.

Joshua prayed to God. In his prayer, find two things Joshua said that showed he loved God and the people. _____

_____

 Thoughts and Observations for Victorious Living

- † What God says is evil, we should not attempt to rebuild.

- † When things do not go as expected and we become discouraged, we should pray to God.

- † The prayers we pray to God should be concerned about God's GREAT NAME.

FOR DISCUSSION

Discuss what Joshua was more concerned about than losing the battle. Such things as being concerned about the enemy winning, their running from the enemy rather than to victory, their own reputation, and the reputation of God.

Dear Parents,

Coach your child they never win when they treasure sin in their heart. See Psalm 66 for more insight in this important principle.

| Day Twelve | **Get Up and 'Fess Up**
Read Joshua 7:10-21 |

✐ **Observations & Questions You Have from the Passage**

_____

_____

_____

_____

_____

_____

_____

_____

Knowing for Yourself

God told Joshua to

_____ instead of

laying on his face.

God told Joshua Israel had

_____ and _____ the covenant He had

made with the people.

> 📍 **FIND IT:** Look up the word "folly" in the dictionary to find out what it means.

What actions did Israel do that were against God? (Check all that apply.)

☐ Stole items God told them to destroy.

☐ Lied about their actions.

☐ Became owner of the stolen items.

Why did the Israelites lose the battle against Ai? _____

_____

God's instruction to Joshua was for Joshua to _____ the people himself before tomorrow.

God told Joshua they must _____ the accursed thing they had stolen, lied about, and put among their own belongings from Jericho.

Why do you think they had to wait until the morning to learn all the facts? _____

Determine how the man who had done wrong was "found out" by numbering in order below:

☐ Sort by Man

☐ Sort by Tribes

☐ Sort by Households in Each Family

☐ Sort by Families in Each Tribe

...

What would happen to the man who was guilty?

_____

What would happen to the stolen items? _____

Who was the man that was selected?

_____

Family Project Idea

Search for the hymn, *Take Time to Be Holy.* Read the lyrics, listen to a performance, and implement ways you could adopt this principle as a family.

What was Achan's reason for taking the items? _____

_____

INTERESTING FACT

There is a difference between sin and trespass. A sin is failing to do the right thing. A trespass is bypassing what you should do, taking a different path.

🖊 Thoughts and Observations for Victorious Living

- † Nothing is ever hidden from God. He sees and knows everything.

- † God wants us to take action to rid us from anything that steals, kills, or destroys.

- † Anything that dishonors or disobeys God must be absolutely destroyed.

- † It is FOOLISH to do something God says we should not do.

- † We want to hide things that are taken wrongfully. God wants to expose them so they can be discarded.

FOR DISCUSSION

Discuss James 1:12–15, relating it to what happened with Achan and strategies to avoid falling into sin.

Dear Parents,

Your child needs to feel "troubled" when they have disobeyed. Meditate on Proverbs 20:30 for greater insight. "Stripes that wound scour away evil. And strokes [reach] the innermost parts."

| Day Thirteen | # The Guilty Are Punished
Read Joshua 7:22–26 |

✎ Observations & Questions You Have from the Passage

_____

_____

_____

_____

_____

_____

Knowing for Yourself

How quickly did the messengers get to Achan's tent? _____

What did they find when they got there?_____

It was (just like/different than) what Achan had told them.

What did the messengers do with what they found?

     A. Took it out of the _____ .

     B. Brought it to _____ and _____ .

     C. Laid it out before _____ .

List what was gathered and taken to the Valley of Achor:

_____   _____   _____

_____   _____   _____

_____   _____   _____

_____   _____   _____

ℹ INTERESTING FACT

Mark 4:22 and Luke 8:17 remind us that nothing
hidden will fail to be exposed.

Joshua asked Achan why he had troubled the people of God.
Why did Joshua ask this question? How had Achan troubled the
people of God? _____

_____

_____

What did the people do to Achan, all who belonged to him, and all
he possessed? _____ and _____

How did they bury Achan and all that he had? _____

_____

The Lord _____ from His fierce anger.

The place is still called The Valley of Achor, which means

_____ .

✏️ Thoughts and Observations for Victorious Living

† God is angry with sin and wickedness. (Psalm 7:11)

† God desires to rid the world of all sin because sin yields death.

† Jesus took the punishment for our sin so that we do not have to pay the penalty of death.

† We should honor God by staying away from sin.

REVIEW THE FOLLOWING OBSERVATIONS AND DISCUSS:

† Achan's sin not only affected him, but it affected his whole family.

† There is no success over the enemy where sin is present.

† Achan confessed his guilt and he was still punished.

† How is the idea of bringing the things Achan took out from hiding similar to the way we need to confess our sins?

† Read 1 John 1:9 and discuss.

Dear Parents,

Fight the battles with your children.
Give them directions and lead the way to
their victory against the enemies they face.

| Day Fourteen | **Let's Try Again**
Read Joshua 8:1-13 |

✐ **Observations & Questions You Have from the Passage**

_____

_____

_____

_____

_____

_____

Knowing for Yourself

The Lord told Joshua to _____ and not to be

_____ .

What were the instructions of the Lord? (Put in order.)

- ☐ Save all the cattle for yourself.
- ☐ Understand I have given you the King, the people, and the land.
- ☐ Take all the people of war.
- ☐ You will conquer Ai.
- ☐ Arise.
- ☐ Go up to Ai.
- ☐ Set up an ambush behind the city.

How many men of war did Joshua get together to go lay behind the city and wait? _____

They were supposed to do what two things when they got behind the city? _____ and
_____

What would the people of the city do? Come out _____ Joshua.

Which way would Joshua and the people run when the city comes out against them? (Toward Ai/Away from Ai)

The people of Ai would think they would _____ the battle because they did before.

When every man from the city of Ai had gone out, what would the people who were waiting and ready to ambush do? _____ upon the city.

Family Project Idea

Act out the Battle of Ai. Include your children's friends and take turns being Joshua's group, Ai's group, and the group waiting beyond the city.

...

When the people had conquered the city, what were they supposed to do to the city? Why? _____
_____

...

Who led the attack and gave the orders for ambush on the city of Ai?
_____

Where did Joshua spend the night? _____

INTERESTING FACT

A definition of the word "fear" is "desire to escape danger." When God told Joshua to not fear, He was telling Joshua to not desire to escape danger. Joshua and his men were at risk and in danger. However, God was with them and had promised to give them success.

Thoughts and Observations for Victorious Living

† When we have no sin in our life/camp, we have nothing to fear and we can know God is with us.

† When we listen to God's instructions and do all He says, we have success.

† The leader must take the lowest position and go between the people and their enemy.

FOR DISCUSSION

Thinking about all the preparation that went into fighting this battle, discuss all the steps to be prepared to fight the battles of life against the enemy (Ephesians 6:12). What can you do as a family and individually to be prepared?

Dear Parents,

Your children will not accomplish
everything they set out to do the first time.
Encourage your children to try again,
depend on the Lord, and look for the win.

Winning the Battle with Ai

Read Joshua 8:14-29

✐ Observations & Questions You Have from the Passage

_____

_____

_____

_____

_____

_____

Knowing for Yourself

When the King of Ai saw _____ in the valley between Ai and Jericho, he hurried and got up early.

The King of Ai and all the men of the city appointed a time to come out of the city and go toward the men Joshua was with in the valley because they knew there were 30,000 men behind the city. (True/False)

Why did Joshua and his men run away from the city?

_____

The men of Ai chased Joshua and the men with him until all the men were out of the city. The gate of the city was (left open/closed).

_____ told Joshua he and his men would win this battle.

When Joshua raised his spear, what did the 30,000 men waiting do? (Check all that apply.)

☐ Set the city on fire

☐ Saved the women and children

☐ Got up slowly and worked slowly

The men of Ai were all out of the city. When they looked back, they: (answer each)

☐ Saw the city on _____ .

☐ (Gained/Lost) courage.

☐ Saw that the Israelites who were going away from the city (turned around/kept going away).

Family Project Idea

Create a comic strip of the battle scene described in Joshua 8:14-29. Some suggestions: a digital comic, a blank comic template printed and drawn, or a piece of posterboard sectioned off in comic strips.

Everyone from the city was killed by the _____ .

Were they to save anything from this city? _____

What happened to the King of Ai? _____

...

✎ Thoughts and Observations for Victorious Living

† God provides victory when we obey His Word and instruction.

† We must not keep anything God says we should destroy.

† Success came because the men followed their leader's instruction and guidance.

FOR DISCUSSION

Discuss how the second battle of Ai and James 4:7-10 compare and contrast with one another. What can you learn from these two passages?

Discuss why the King of Ai was killed. Include in the discussion why it was necessary to utterly destroy this city. With God's view of winning over the enemy by totally getting rid of the enemy, what can be learned about a strategy to get rid of the enemies in your life? Take some time to identify the enemies you face.

A WORD ABOUT VICTORY

Victory is defined as *success in a contest*. The children of Israel fought the Battle of Ai twice. They were in two contests. The first contest was lost because of sin and trespass. The second battle was won because of God's presence, which triumphed over the enemy.

The victorious fight was real for Joshua and the 30,000 men with him. They had to carry the swords. They had to get in place, stay out of the enemy's view, and be ready to "do their thing" when they were signaled.

Just because God has determined the win is inevitable does not mean there is not a battle. It does not mean the battle is not real. It does not mean there will not be pain, difficulty, and loss. Instead, **it is the assurance the victory is ours, which enables us to keep fighting.**

Romans 8, a great chapter for the New Testament believer, tells us the victory is won. It tells us we are *more than conquers through Jesus Christ who loved us and gave himself for us*. This statement does not make the battles go away. It does not make the struggle disappear. It does not make the contest nonexistent. Instead, this chapter tells us we will suffer hardship. We will have difficulty. The trouble and distress we experience is real. At times, we will feel like our life is hanging by a thread. However, our current feeling is not the end of the story. *The end of the story is that we will be victorious.*

The reasoning of Romans 8 is encouraging to those who are struggling with the pressures of life, torments of Satan, and their own natural tendencies. The chapter tells us we are **victorious through Christ Jesus who loved us and gave himself for us.** We are assured of our victory. Romans 8:31 says, *"If God be for us, who can be against us?"*

It does not matter who or what we are fighting against. No matter how troubled, distressed, or perilous the times we encounter are, we know that Christ has won the victory for us. Nothing can separate us from the love of God which is in Christ Jesus. With this assurance of victory, we stay connected to Jesus, OUR VICTORY.

NOTES

_____

_____

_____

_____

_____

_____

_____

_____

_____

_____

Dear Parents,

Your children see your example and follow your lead. Even if they don't seem to care now, they are paying attention. Demonstrate before them a reverence, honor, and priority for the Lord in all the ways you interact with them and others.

| Day Sixteen | **Give Honor Where Honor is Due**

Read Joshua 8:30-35 |

✏ Observations & Questions You Have from the Passage

_____

_____

_____

_____

_____

_____

_____

Knowing for Yourself

After the city of Ai was taken, what did Joshua do first?

    A. Go to sleep.

    B. Build an altar to the Lord.

    C. Shake everyone's hand.

    D. Take a bath.

They were to offer _____ offerings and
_____ offerings on the altar Joshua built.

Joshua wrote a copy of the _____ on the stones.

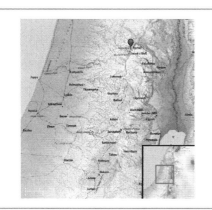

FIND IT: Find Mount Ebal and Mount Gerizim on the map

What were the children of Israel doing while Joshua was writing?

☐ Sleeping

☐ Watching

☐ Shaking everyone's hand

☐ Taking a bath

Bible Memorization Challenge

The Ten Commandments Exodus 20:3-17

Who was in this scene? (Check all that apply.)

☐ Women

☐ Children

☐ Elders

☐ Officers

☐ Priests

☐ The King of Ai

☐ Judges

☐ Strangers

Half of the people stood by Mount _____ and half by

Mount _____ .

Family Project Idea

Use craft stones to help your family memorize the Ten Commandments. Write a commandment on each stone. Leave them at unique places throughout the house. The person who finds the stone places it somewhere else to be found by another family member. Have each family member locate and re-locate all 10 stones throughout the playing time.

Joshua read all the words of the law, including the _____ and
_____ .

Who was responsible to listen to all Joshua read? _____
_____

INTERESTING FACT
Burnt offerings were to represent an offering
of tribute. Peace offerings were to represent
an offering of friendship or well-being.

✎ Thoughts and Observations for Victorious Living

† Victories in our life should cause us to desire more of
God's Word.

† Each individual is responsible to listen to the Word of God.

† Blessing comes as we read, hear, and heed God's Word.

FOR DISCUSSION
Discuss 2 Timothy 3:16-17. Define what Scripture
is. List the ways it is necessary, useful, and
beneficial. Explain the reason reading, hearing,
and understanding God's Word is so important
individually and as a family, if you are utilizing
Scripture correctly.

Dear Parents,

It was the reputation of God's power in the lives of the children of Israel that made the Gibeonites want to be their friends. Teach your children to thoroughly investigate with whom they become close friends. Some friends may not be truthful about who they really are and where they are coming from. Teach your children to be cautious. Use this account in the book of Joshua to have this discussion.

| Day Seventeen | **The Great Deception**
Read Joshua 9:1-15 |

✎ **Observations & Questions You Have from the Passage**

_____

_____

_____

_____

_____

_____

_____

_____

Knowing for Yourself

When the kings of the lands around Ai heard all the children of Israel were doing, they decided to:

☐ Fight on the same side with Joshua and the people.

☐ Fight against Joshua and the people.

Consider praying to God to know who you should be friends with. Psalm 1:1 gives a good guideline for the sort of people to avoid.

The people of Gibeon heard what Joshua had done to Jericho and Ai, so they made a plan to:

☐ Tell Joshua they lived close by and make peace with the Israelites.

☐ Tell Joshua they lived far away, had come a really long way, and wanted to be their servants.

What did the Gibeonites make to look old? _____

_____

_____

What did the people of Gibeon want Joshua and the people to make with them? _____

Joshua met with the men and asked them who they were and where they had come from. What did the people tell Joshua?

_____

What had the people heard that made them come to Joshua?

_____

_____

What did the men do to "prove" that they had come from a long way away? _____

_____

Joshua and the men had a suspicion the people may be deceiving them, because they asked, "What if . . . ?" Did they ask God?

_____

_____

_____

What did Joshua do with the men who had come?

☐ Sent them away.

☐ Made a covenant with them.

INTERESTING FACT

A covenant is an agreement. It is like a promise. Some versions of the Bible use the word league. It still means they agreed to live together without fighting.

✏ Thoughts and Observations for Victorious Living

† When something doesn't seem right and you have a small question inside, you probably should ask God.

† God's power is displayed unto the children of men and in all His acts.

FOR DISCUSSION

Discuss the word *deception*. How did the Gibeonites deceive Joshua? Are there ways in your life or family that you deceive?

Dear Parents,

This passage of Scripture is a great teaching opportunity. There may have been times when you, as a leader, didn't make the best decision and your child got upset with you. Encourage your child that when you mess up in your decisions, you always try to make the best of the situation in which you find yourself. For example, the leaders in this passage made the inclusion of the Gibeonites to serve the people and lessen their work.

The Truth Always Comes Out

Read Joshua 9:16-27

✎ **Observations & Questions You Have from the Passage**

_____

_____

_____

_____

_____

_____

_____

_____

Knowing for Yourself

How long did it take to hear the Gibeonites had deceived Joshua and his men? _____

How long did it take Joshua and his men to go to Gibeon where the men were from? _____

Why didn't Joshua and the leaders destroy the people from Gibeon?

_____

The people were (happy/upset) about the decision of the leaders of Israel.

INTERESTING FACT

A name represents what a person is known by. A name is their reputation. We go to "name brand" stores because they have a reputation we want to experience. The leaders of the children of Israel had promised by the name of the Lord (reputation of God) not to destroy these people with whom they had made an agreement. Therefore, it was because of God's name they protected them, kept the people as servants, and did not destroy them.

Whose wrath would be upon Israel if they killed or hurt the people of Gibeon? _____

The leaders of Israel determined the Gibeonites would be: Cutters of _____ and drawers of _____ .

...

Joshua called the Gibeonites and spoke to them the following: (Put in order)

☐ You will continually be slaves to us.

☐ Why did you deceive us?

☐ You will cut wood and draw water for the house of God.

☐ You will be cursed.

The Gibeonites told Joshua it was because they were _____
that they lied.

The Gibeonites fought against Joshua. (True/False)

The people of Israel wanted to kill the Gibeonites.

Who stopped them? _____

Who did the people of Gibeon do their work for? _____

...

 Thoughts and Observations for Victorious Living

- † God wants us to keep our promises ALWAYS.
- † God wants us to ask Him BEFORE we make promises.
- † Everyone will work to carry on God's work.
- † God used the bad decision of Joshua and the leaders for their good by providing additional people to help with the duties that were needed.

FOR DISCUSSION

Read and discuss Romans 8:28-29. Talk about how God made the lies of the Gibeonites, the bad decisions of the leaders, and the deception that was believed to all work together for good.

Dear Parents,

It takes great stamina and energy to help your children in fighting their battles. When your children call out for your help, show up. As you pray and look to the Lord for help, He will give you all that is needed. After all is said and done, you'll see it is the Lord who fought for your children and He prevailed.

| Day Nineteen | **The Lord Fights for Israel** |
| | Read Joshua 10:1-14 |

✐ Observations & Questions You Have from the Passage

_____

_____

_____

_____

_____

_____

_____

Knowing for Yourself

Where was the king from who had heard Joshua had defeated Ai and made peace with the Gibeonites? _____

Why were the kings around Gibeon fearful? _____

Gibeon was considered a _____ city. All the men of Gibeon were _____ .

The king of Jerusalem called the kings of surrounding cities to come up and help him.

Which city do the kings belong to? Draw a line to match the city with the king.

Debir	Jerusalem
Param	Hebron
Adonizedec	Jarmuth
Hoham	Lachish
Japhia	Eglon

The king of Jerusalem wanted the other four kings to help him fight _____ because they had made peace with

_____ .

Did the kings go together to make war? (Yes/No)

The kings camped outside of _____ .

The people called for _____ to come help.

Joshua and all the mighty men stayed home. (True/False)

What did the Lord tell Joshua about this battle?

☐ Nothing.

☐ Fear them not; I have delivered them into your hands.

Joshua went (slowly/quickly) to help.

> 📍 **FIND IT: Locate a map that shows all the cities mentioned in this passage and trace the path of this battle.**

The Lord caused the men of the five cities coming against Israel to _____ before them.

Joshua asked the Lord to make the sun stand still. Did it happen? (Yes/No)

There was never a day like it before or after when the Lord
_____ to the voice of a man.

Who fought for Israel? _____

Thoughts and Observations for Victorious Living

† God gives victory over enemies who come against us.

† God gives power and strength to keep going despite distance and terrain.

† The Lord knows what the outcome of everything is. We can have confidence in God.

FOR DISCUSSION

Discuss how it is important to help others we are friends with. Talk about what Israel did for Gibeon that showed they were friends. Discuss real-life scenarios where you can demonstrate friendship to others.

Discuss why "the Lord listened to the voice of a man." Talk about what was unique about Joshua. How can you learn from Joshua's life so your prayers can be heard by God?

Dear Parents,

In what ways are you leading your children to victory? Are you giving them direction to defeat their enemies? Are you fighting the battle with them? Are you interceding with the Lord for the sun not to go down in their life? Are you trapping the enemy so they cannot exercise control over your children? Take Joshua as an example of how to help your children live victoriously.

| | **Be Strong and Courageous**
Read Joshua 10:15-27 |

✎ Observations & Questions You Have from the Passage

_____

_____

_____

_____

_____

_____

_____

Knowing for Yourself

Where did Joshua return? _____

Where did the five kings go?

☐ Back to their cities.

☐ To hide in a cave.

☐ They were killed.

What did Joshua do to the five kings?

☐ Had stones rolled over the cave opening.

☐ Broke the king's swords.

☐ Sent the kings presents.

Joshua told the people to keep going after the people of the cities and not allow them to enter their cities. Why?

- ☐ The Lord had delivered them into their hand.
- ☐ The kings were weak and tired.
- ☐ The people were hungry.

When the battle was over, where did Israel camp? _____

Everyone talked bad about the children of Israel. (True/False)

Who decided to take the kings out of the cave and have them killed?

_____

...

Joshua _____ the kings and _____ them on a tree until it was _____ .

Where were the kings taken after they died?

- ☐ Back to their cities for burial.
- ☐ Back in the cave.

What did they put over the mouth of the cave? _____

 INTERESTING FACT

Luke 6:45 tells us we speak what is in our heart (inner man). If we have God's words in our inner man, we will speak them.

Thoughts and Observations for Victorious Living

† When we've heard from the Lord, we can encourage others.

† We have strength and courage for the battle when we are sure God will destroy our enemies and give us victory.

† Victory is sure when God is directing the way.

FOR DISCUSSION

Read Joshua 10:25. Do you remember another time in the book of Joshua those words were used? Where was it? Why do you think Joshua was able to tell the people this message? Joshua had heard these same words from God at the beginning of the book. The words had gotten into his heart. Now they were being spoken from his mouth. Look up Psalm 19:14. How had Joshua put this verse into practice? How can you put this verse into practice in your life? We please God when we speak to Him and others what He has spoken.

A WORD ABOUT MEDITATION

Meditation is *thinking about something deeply* including *considering it with extreme detail*. We rarely have time to think these days. Our life is fast-paced. There is always something to do, watch, listen to, take part in, and attend. We rarely have time to focus on thinking about the details of God, His Word, and His works.

There have always been distractions, though in King David's day when he was writing and thinking about Psalm 119, he didn't have a cell phone to check in the middle of the night or first thing when he woke up. He didn't have immediate answers to his questions via the Internet. Instead, he did things like this:

- † Meditate all day on God's laws. (Psalm 119:97)
- † Wake up early for the purpose of meditating on God's promises. (Psalm 119:148)

To accomplish the meditation of God's Word, we may have to do things differently than we've been doing them. Thinking deeply about the *works of God*, *ways of God*, and *wonders of God* will enable us to hide His Word in our heart that we may not sin against God. We will be spared from missing the target by ignorance. So let's be "in the know" of God's Word. Here are some suggestions for helping us to meditate on God's Word:

- † Write Scripture verses on index cards. Put them where you will see them, such as in your vehicle, where you get ready, or on the refrigerator.
- † Set an alarm on your phone to rehearse the verse routinely throughout the day.

<blockquote>

      ✝   Set a goal of knowing the verse by a certain date. Have an accountability partner and reward system.

As we set a regular habit of meditating on the Word of God, we will see His magnificence with greater detail and our mouths will overflow with encouragement to others.

</blockquote>

NOTES

_____

_____

_____

_____

_____

_____

_____

_____

_____

_____

_____

_____

_____

_____

Dear Parents,

Teaching your child endurance is very important. Endurance means that you keep going when you feel like quitting. Joshua 10 doesn't give any indication of whether Joshua felt like quitting or was energized to keep going. When we endure, we go on no matter how we feel. Joshua may have had to remind himself, "No man shall stand before you" to keep his endurance up. Remind your child that sometimes they will need to talk to themselves and remind themselves to keep going even when they feel like quitting.

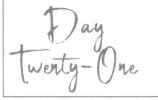

| Day twenty-One | **The Fight Continues**
Read Joshua 10:28-37 |

✎ Observations & Questions You Have from the Passage

_____

_____

_____

_____

_____

_____

_____

Knowing for Yourself

Joshua took a break from all the fighting because he was tired. (True/False)

How did Joshua destroy the people of Makkedah? _____

_____

Did he leave anyone left alive from the city of Makkedah? (Yes/No)

He destroyed the King of Makkedah like he had destroyed the King of _____ .

After Makkedah, what was the next city Joshua utterly destroyed?

_____

 INTERESTING FACT

There's a slight difference between utterly destroy and smote. To utterly destroy something is to exterminate it and render it useless, whereas to smite/smote something is to attack it or go against it. Joshua did both to the cities and the people he fought against in Joshua 10.

Who caused Joshua to win all these battles and utterly destroy all these cities? _____

Lachish was destroyed on which day of these battles? _____

Who came up to help Lachish? _____ Was the help successful for Lachish? (Yes/No)

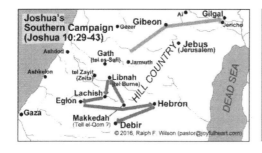

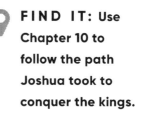 **FIND IT: Use Chapter 10 to follow the path Joshua took to conquer the kings.**

After Lachish, Joshua moved on to Eglon. What happened at Eglon?

☐ Joshua lost the battle.
☐ The people of Israel got too tired to keep going.
☐ They fought against it and won.

What city did they go to next after Eglon? _____

Was anyone left remaining in any of the cities Joshua and his men fought against? (Yes/No)

...

✎ Thoughts and Observations for Victorious Living

† When God gives you work to do, keep doing it until it is complete.

† We must not allow anything to remain in our lives that would hinder our relationship with God.

† God gives strength to do the battling He has prescribed.

† God gives victory in the battles.

FOR DISCUSSION

Discuss how Joshua used a sword to fight and win against enemy. In the New Testament we are told to use the sword of the Lord, which is the Word of God. How is this similar? How can we learn and use the Bible to fight the battles of life?

Dear Parents,

Joshua kept doing what God had told him to do. Encourage your child to keep doing the right thing even when it's hard, when it seems everything and everybody is against you, and when you are tired. God rewards with victory those who continue to do what He has instructed.

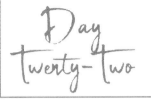

The Enemy Unifies to Attack

Read Joshua 10:38-11:5

✎ **Observations & Questions You Have from the Passage**

_____

_____

_____

_____

_____

_____

_____

Knowing for Yourself

After Joshua had left Hebron, what city did they destroy next?

_____

Who commanded Joshua to destroy all these cities and kill all these people? _____

Who fought for Israel? _____

After they left Debir, where did they go? _____

_____

Bible Memorization Challenge

Romans 8:31-37

God had given the children of Israel speed, power, and success in destroying all these cities. (True/False)

After some time, King _____ of Hazor got some other kings together to fight against Joshua.

...

There were _____ cities and _____ other people groups/regions who came out against Joshua.

There were just a few people who came out against Joshua. (True/False)

Where did all the people go to meet against Joshua? _____

The people had come out to _____ against the people of Israel.

Family Project Idea

Look up Proverbs 11:21 and write the verse at the top of a large sheet of paper. Then list the groups of kings who came together and could not win in the center. At the bottom of the large paper, write a family motto that will remind you though the enemy joins together against you, because you belong to God, you will win.

...

FIND IT: Use His Strength is Perfect by Steven Curtis Chapman

Review the lyrics and listen to a performance.
Pray * Read * Write

All you're learning about God's perfect strength.

Thoughts and Observations for Victorious Living

† God requires our footing to be stable and steadfast on different types of ground and terrain.

† Though we fight and battle against sin, the Lord God who is the same yesterday, today, and forever fights for us.

† We have speed, power, and success in our lives when we do all that God commands us to do in His Word.

† Nothing can ultimately have victory over the Lord.

FOR DISCUSSION

Discuss how Joshua used a sword to fight and win against the enemy. In the New Testament we are told to use the sword of the Lord, which is the Word of God. How is this similar? How can we learn and use the Bible to fight the battles of life?

Dear Parents,

Whether you are a first generation follower of God or a multi-generational follower of God, it is important to hear the Lord's commands and to do them. Matthew 12:50 reminds us that it is in doing the will of God that we are considered to be in the family of God. It is being in the family of God that makes us on the winning team.

	The War Continues
	Read Joshua 11:6-23

✍ Observations & Questions You Have from the Passage

_____

_____

_____

_____

_____

_____

_____

Knowing for Yourself

What did the Lord tell Joshua?

☐ Watch out for them, there are so many. Do your best.

☐ Be not afraid because of them, for tomorrow I will cause you to win.

What further instructions did God give?

_____ their horses

_____ their chariots

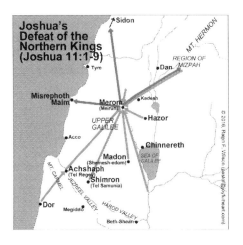

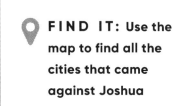

FIND IT: Use the map to find all the cities that came against Joshua

How did Joshua come to meet the people at the waters of Merom?

☐ Suddenly

☐ Slowly

Who caused Joshua to win? _____

Where did Joshua chase the people? _____

What did Joshua do to their chariots? _____

What did Joshua do to their horses? _____

Why did Joshua do these things to their chariots and horses?

_____

What was done to Hazor?

_____

What was spared from the cities?

_____

How much land did Joshua take?

☐ A little

☐ A lot

☐ None

Family Project Idea

Think about what the scene of the battle looked like. Draw a picture as a family of the scene. As you draw, talk about how Joshua may have felt and the reason God was giving Joshua victory.

_____

Joshua made war with the _____ a long time.

What city and people group was not destroyed? _____

...

What was the purpose of defeating all these kings and conquering their land?

☐ God had given the land to the children of Israel as an inheritance.

☐ God wanted to scare people.

...

 Thoughts and Observations for Victorious Living

†   We must make ineffective and burn anything that opposes God and His ways.

†   We must keep going until all our enemies are defeated. Then comes rest.

> **FOR DISCUSSION**
>
> Discuss how the Bible passage explains that Moses had told Joshua what to do. Moses got his information from God. Joshua got his information from Moses. The people got their information from Joshua. What can you learn and implement from this chain of command?

Dear Parents,

Celebrate the wins of your children.
Encourage your children to be people
who are flexible and able to withstand
all sorts of terrain in the battles of
life. Role play scenarios of conflict
to help them practice preparedness.

 **Day twenty-Four**

The Kings Defeated

Read Joshua 12:1-24

✍ Observations & Questions You Have from the Passage

_____

_____

_____

_____

_____

_____

Knowing for Yourself

What leader of the cities did the children of Israel destroy?

_____

Why was this leader chosen to be destroyed? _____

_____

Verses 1-6 of Chapter 12 state the territory Moses conquered and gave to the Reubenites, Gadites, and half tribe of Manasseh. Where was this territory relative to the Jordan River?

- ☐ West side
- ☐ East side

Joshua conquered territories on which side of the Jordan?

    ☐ West side

    ☐ East side

What was the terrain of the land Joshua led the children to fight on?

_____

_____

How many kings were defeated?

_____

Family Project Idea

Keep a record of enemies you as a family have conquered. Identify enemies in the life of your family, pray for God's strategy to overcome them, and record the victory when it comes.

_____

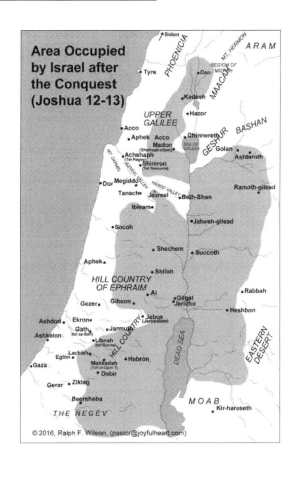

Area Occupied by Israel after the Conquest (Joshua 12-13)

©2016, Ralph F. Wilson, (pastor@joyfulheart.com)

INTERESTING FACT

Interesting Fact – In sports, a player is usually excellent in one position. The player can play in more than one position and do well. However, he/she is most skilled and trained in one position. In the battles Joshua led to conquer all these kings, the troops *played* excellently in all positions. The playing field was different for each kingdom they conquered and they won all the battles.

✏ Thoughts and Observations for Victorious Living

† We can defeat anything if we get rid of the leadership. (Think about things that control the sin in your life. If you get rid of what is leading that sin, you can defeat the sin.)

† God takes territories away from sinners and gives them to His people.

FOR DISCUSSION

Discuss how you can be prepared to stand and fight the battles of your life and the life of your family no matter the terrain of the place of combat. What preparations can you make to ensure victory for yourself and that of your family?

Dear Parents,

God had a work for Joshua to do just as He has a work for you to do. Ephesians 2:10 reminds us we are working for the Lord doing what He has planned since the beginning for us to do. Keep getting your instructions from the Lord for your work, though you are old and advanced in years.

Reconciling the Remainder

Read Joshua 13:1-21

✎ **Observations & Questions You Have from the Passage**

_____

_____

_____

_____

_____

_____

Knowing for Yourself

What did the Lord tell Joshua?

☐ You are old but still strong. There is still much land to possess.

☐ You are old and have lived a long time. There is much land to possess.

What land was still left to possess? _____ and

_____

Joshua 13:3 states that there were five Philistine rulers, but how many were listed?

_____ _____ _____

_____ _____ _____

FIND IT: Look at the map on Day 24. Locate the
following lands left to be conquered – Bashan, Geshur,
and Aphek. What do you observe about their location to
one another?

How many tribes would be getting land on the west of the Jordan?
_____ tribes and _____ tribe of Manasseh

Who gave the tribes of Reuben and Gad their inheritance?
_____

...

_____

Family Project Idea

Strategize how you would go about conquering the other
lands. Use the map of the lands on Day 24 to view where
the lands were that were still left to be conquered.

_____

...

Which people groups were the children of Israel unable to expel
from the land? _____ and _____

Which tribe would not get a land inheritance? _____

What would the inheritance of Levi be? _____

Thoughts and Observations for Victorious Living

† There is still much work to be done for the Lord, even if someone is old and has lived a long time.

...

FOR DISCUSSION

Discuss the reason the tribe of Levi received no land inheritance. It was said that "the Lord was their portion." Review Deuteronomy 10:8-9 for the backstory. Discuss if you would have liked to have been part of the tribe of Levi or not.

A WORD ABOUT RECKONING

To reckon something means to "get it in order" or "consider." Joshua took the time to get in order what was left to be conquered. He considered, with the Lord's guidance, what was remaining. He wanted to know what else would have to be "paid" to get what was coming to him and the children of Israel. He wanted to know what work was left to be done.

There is a New Testament passage of Scripture similar to this principle. It is found in Romans 8:18. One version reads, "For I consider that the sufferings of this present time are not worth comparing with the glory that is to be revealed to us."

Joshua considered the land that was left to be conquered. He was willing to go on, though he was "old and stricken in years," so that he could attain the land that God had promised him and the children of Israel. As New Testament believers, we consider the glory of God that is yet to be experienced by us. We go on through "the sufferings of this present time" because the value of what will be attained is far greater than the difficulty today.

At the time of Joshua 13, they spent some time reconciling what was left to be conquered, what cost would be paid, and rehearsing what the promises of God were to them.

Today, as we consider what is promised to us, what glory is yet to be revealed to us, let us take the time to reconcile what cost must be paid. Romans 8 says there will be suffering. It claims difficulty in the days ahead. We are assured, however, when we consider the cost, the glory far outweighs the cost.

Take some time to make a list of the glory that is yet to be revealed to you and your family. Make a list of the "suffering" that must be endured to obtain it. Consider how the glory is of so much more value than the suffering.

NOTES

_____

_____

_____

_____

_____

_____

_____

_____

_____

_____

_____

_____

_____

Dear Parents,

The passages of God's Word are written for our examples. See Romans 15:9. All the places, kings, territories, and details were written to remind us that God is a God of detail. When it comes to our lives and the lives of your children, you appreciate the detail. Be encouraged yourself over the details given in God's Word. Encourage your child not to loathe the long, detailed account. Listen and try to discern the reason God included it in the Bible, what we can learn, and how it teaches us to endure to the end.

A Realization of Blessing

Read Joshua 13:22-33

✏ Observations & Questions You Have from the Passage

_____

_____

_____

_____

_____

_____

Knowing for Yourself

Who did the children of Israel kill with the sword? _____

What was his occupation?

_____

Moses gave inheritance to the tribe of Reuben according to their

_____ .

Moses gave inheritance to the tribe of Gad according to their

_____ .

Bible Memorization Challenge

2 Corinthians 6:17-18

Moses gave inheritance to the half tribe of _____ .

...

 FIND IT: Look up "soothsayer" in a dictionary or concordance. What kind of person is a soothsayer? Why was it important this person be killed?

...

Who received half Gilead, Ashtaroth, and Edrei? _____

The lands Moses gave as inheritance were on the (east/west) of the Jordan.

Unto the tribe of _____ Moses gave not any land because _____ would be their inheritance.

...

Thoughts and Observations for Victorious Living

- † God removes from the wicked to bless His people.
- † We must rid from our presence anyone who speaks divination or speaks against our Lord God.

FOR DISCUSSION

Discuss Psalm 16. How do the conquering of the land and "lines in pleasant places" mentioned in Psalm 16 correspond to each other? How were the wicked of the nations destroyed? How were the righteous preserved? Identify and discuss habits you can learn from this psalm. Put them into practice so that you and your family have a right perspective and appreciation for all God has provided for you.

Dear Parents,

Use this story to teach your child that trusting God is worth it. Encourage your child to keep trusting God for His promises. Caleb had heard 45 years earlier he would get a portion of the land. He was ready to take possession of it then. But his "untrusting" companions won out and died in the wilderness. Caleb, however, had kept trusting God for the promise. Now, Caleb was realizing the promise for himself. He was about to possess the land after 45 years of trusting.

Day twenty-Seven

God's Promise Realized

Read Joshua 14:1-15

✎ Observations & Questions You Have from the Passage

_____

_____

_____

_____

_____

_____

Knowing for Yourself

Who helped Joshua distribute the land to the children of Israel?

_____

Which of the fathers had their tribe divided into two parts?

_____

Who instructed them to divide the land? _____

Caleb came to Joshua. Which tribe was he from? _____

Caleb and _____ had been two of the original spies when the children of Israel went to check out the land about conquering it.

How old was Caleb when he went to spy the land? _____

Who did Caleb wholly follow? _____

How old was Caleb when he was talking to Moses? _____

...

Caleb wanted Joshua to give him the mountain and with the help of _____ he would drive out the people from the land.

What place did Joshua give Caleb? _____

What was the reason for Caleb to get this place? _____

The land had _____ from war.

...

INTERESTING FACT

Caleb was 85 years old and said he was as strong as he was when Moses sent him to spy out the land 45 years earlier. God had kept Caleb strong all these years. He had given Caleb the strength to keep going and to fight. Psalm 18:25-30 provides a graphic illustration of how those who trust in God can do amazing things. They can do things like jump over a wall . . . all because they believe God's perfect promises.

✏ Thoughts and Observations for Victorious Living

† God rewards faithfulness, trust, and obedience. However, it may take 45 years for us to obtain it and even then, we may still have to fight for it.

† God never forgets a person's faithfulness.

† God is faithful and keeps His promises.

FOR DISCUSSION

Discuss what it means to "wait on the Lord." Include in the discussion the benefit of waiting on the Lord. What makes waiting on the Lord difficult? How did Caleb wait on the Lord? What are some strategies you could identify and use to help you wait on the Lord? Use Joshua 14 and Isaiah 40:31 to enrich the discussion. Determine at least one thing you could practice that encourages you to keep waiting.

Dear Parents,

Giving by lot and establishing boundaries in your family are important principles. Be sure each of your children know what they posses and what is within their "power" to control. Encourage them to take possession of what is theirs, establish themselves, and maintain their responsibilities. As they increase in age and wisdom, enlarge their boundaries.

Enlarging the Borders

Read Joshua 15:1-15

✍ Observations & Questions You Have from the Passage

_____

_____

_____

_____

_____

_____

Knowing for Yourself

What was the most southern border that was the lot to the tribe of Judah? _____

Which was the sea that bordered Judah on the south? _____

What is another name for Jerusalem? _____

Caleb received part of the land that was given to the children of which tribe? _____

What was the name of the city given to Caleb? _____

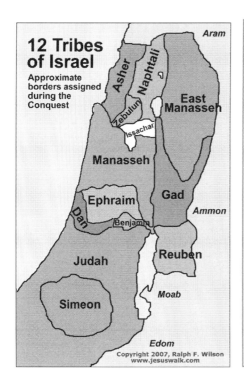

FIND IT:

Search online for a map that shows the following cities: Hebron and Debir. Locate where they are on the map. Discuss why you think Caleb conquered Hebron before he conquered Debir.

...

Who did Caleb drive out of the city? _____, _____, and _____ . These were children of _____ .

What was the next city Caleb went up to? _____

What was the city's name later changed to? _____

The city of Debir before was named _____ .

...

✏️ Thoughts and Observations for Victorious Living

†   God is specific in His boundaries and borders.

†   God has limits He wants us to stay within.

†   God gives us things we can possess while we live on earth.

FOR DISCUSSION

Discuss the prayer found in 1 Chronicles 4:9–10. What was Jabez's prayer? Why did Jabez desire God to answer this prayer? How did God answer the prayer of Jabez? Discuss how Caleb may have prayed for God to enlarge his territory. How did Caleb's territory get enlarged? In what ways are we responsible to do some "work" to get the borders enlarged? Compose a family prayer about enlarging your center of influence for good and to display God's light wherever you dwell.

Dear Parents,

Caleb asked his daughter what she wanted when she came to him. He listened and considered if he could provide. When your child comes to you, be sure to listen to what they ask, consider if you can provide, and act accordingly. Remember, no matter how old they get, they're still your children. God gave them to you to love, to nurture, and to provide for.

| Day twenty-Nine | **A Special Request**
Read Joshua 15:16-47 |

✍ **Observations & Questions You Have from the Passage**

_____

_____

_____

_____

_____

_____

_____

_____

Knowing for Yourself

Did Caleb conquer Debir himself? (Yes/No)

Caleb declared that whoever could conquer Kirjath-sepher, he would give his daughter to be his _____ .

Who conquered the city of Kirjath-sepher? _____

How was he related to Caleb? _____

What was the name of Caleb's daughter he gave to be the wife of the one who conquered the land? _____

Whose idea was it for Caleb to give the new couple a spring of water?
_____

...

Family Project Idea

Write a poem or song that would represent Achsah's response to receiving the springs of water she had requested.

...

 INTERESTING FACT

Joshua 15 tells us places are called by more than one name. Multiple times throughout the Bible, people have been called by different names. Here are some examples:

Abram – Abraham

Sarai – Sarah

Jacob – Israel

Simon – Peter

Naomi – Mara

Saul – Paul

Thoughts and Observations for Victorious Living

† We should be willing to ask for things that we need.

† We please God when we ask for things we need. (Hebrews 11:6)

...

FOR DISCUSSION

Discuss Hebrews 11:6. How do we come to God? What can we do to please God? What does it mean to diligently seek God? Create a strategy of victory you can do in your family to live by faith, ask God for what you need, please Him always, and come to Him consistently.

Dear Parents,

Do not be discouraged when you do not seem to win all the battles. The children of Israel lived with people they could not conquer. Inform your children they may not always be in agreement with everyone they have close connections. Just as the children of Israel had to learn to get along with others, we can too. See Romans 12:18 for further study.

Day Thirty	## God Provides Plentifully Read Joshua 15:48–63

✐ Observations & Questions You Have from the Passage

_____

_____

_____

_____

_____

_____

_____

_____

_____

_____

Knowing for Yourself

What was the city name Kirjath-sannah another name for?

_____

What was another name for the city of Hebron? _____

Why do you think there were only six cities in the wilderness area?

_____

Family Project Idea

Thinking about the Jebusites continuing to be in the land of Jerusalem and the children of Israel moving in to live among them, read John 17:14-19.

Answer the following questions:

    †   Why does the world hate followers of God?
    †   Why are followers of God not of the world?
    †   What makes Christians different from the people of the world?

Role play scenarios of how following the Word of God makes you different from people who follow the world's system.

...

What people group inhabited Jerusalem? _____

Could the children of Israel drive out this people group from Jerusalem? (Yes/No)

What happened to the people group? _____

...

 FIND IT: Locate a map of all the cities of Judah. Find as many of the city names listed in Joshua 15 on the map as possible. What observations do you make about the land, terrain, and/or city locations?

✐ Thoughts and Observations for Victorious Living

† God is faithful to provide His people with cities and villages
to call their own.

FOR DISCUSSION

Caleb shows up once the land is conquered.
Caleb was part of the tribe of Judah. Why do
you think Judah got the first land distribution
on the west side of the Jordan? There were
already distributions of Reuben, Gad, and half
the tribe of Manasseh on the east side of the
Jordan. What would be your reason for the tribe
of Judah to have gotten the first distribution on
the west side?

A WORD ABOUT THE FAITHFULNESS OF GOD

The song, "Great Is Thy Faithfulness," is a loved classic among followers of God. What exactly is God's faithfulness? Why is it so great?

Take the time to look up the lyrics of this song. Whether you are familiar with the song or not, reading hymn lyrics enlarges your understanding and captures your attention toward God.

Loyalty is another way to explain the faithfulness of God. He is a companion who never gives up, a caregiver, and our provider. God is steadfast and unchanging in His trustworthiness. He stays close by us through hard times and good times.

The greatness of God's faithfulness can be expressed in many ways. God has a huge store of greatness. He is great in mercy and compassion. He has a huge ability to suffer a long time on behalf of someone else. He can take a lot of "junk" and does not abandon them.

Psalm 89 tells us so beautifully of God's faithfulness through displays in nature. The sun and moon are used as a daily visual reminder of God's faithfulness. Take some time to meditate on Psalm 89. Experience how the faithfulness of God will remain as sure, steady, and expected as the sun rising in the morning and the display of the moon at night.

Probably the most cheering news of God's faithfulness is the presence of God that will never leave or forsake. Deuteronomy 31:6 are God's direct words through Moses that God would never leave or forsake Joshua. The verse is rehearsed again in the New Testament, in Hebrews 13:5, encouraging the follower of Christ. The words are meant to spur the follower of God on to confidence in God because God is loyal to them to never leave or forsake them.

We could not leave the subject of faithfulness without mentioning Isaiah 41:10. We are instructed in this text to be strong and of good courage. God is with us, never leaving us, and not only that, but He is holding us up by His hand that gets things done. He is working on our behalf.

This brings us to the final Scripture for instruction about God's faithfulness in the life of a believer. It is God who works in us both to want to do and to do what is pleasing in His eyes. Philippians 2:13 conveys this quality of the faithfulness of God.

Think back over Joshua 15. This chapter is a culmination of what God has been doing in the life of His people for over 40 years. God has been working to give them this land. It is in this chapter we see God distributing to them what He has had for them for a long time. God is faithful to do what He has promised.

GREAT IS THE FAITHFULNESS OF GOD!

NOTES

_____

_____

_____

_____

_____

Dear Parents,

Weaknesses are real. God promises His grace is sufficient in our weakness. (2 Corinthians 12:9) Your children need to hear your testimony of the grace of God present in your life. When your children hear how the grace of God helps you, your children will learn how to deal with weakness God's way – using His grace.

Day thirty-One

Servants Will Always Exist

Read Joshua 16:1-10

✐ **Observations & Questions You Have from the Passage**

_____

_____

_____

_____

_____

_____

_____

_____

_____

_____

Knowing for Yourself

Manasseh and Ephraim were the children of _____ .

Manasseh and Ephraim refused to take their inheritance. (True/False)

Bible Memorization Challenge

Psalm 100

In which city did the Canaanites dwell? _____

What happened to the Canaanites? _____

Ephraim, the children of Israel, are slaves to the Canaanites. (True/False)

 INTERESTING FACT

Just as Canaanites served Ephraim, we should serve God. Psalm 100:2 says we should serve Him with gladness.

What do you think slaves in the Bible would have experienced?

_____

...

 FIND IT: On a map locate the Jordan River and determine if all of it is in the land assigned to Ephraim and Manasseh. What do you think about what you find?

...

✎ Thoughts and Observations for Victorious Living

†   God makes His own rules in the division of the land.

†   God's people receive favor from the Lord and He takes care of them.

FOR DISCUSSION

Discuss your thoughts about God allowing the Canaanites to stay in the land. How do you think they were a hindrance to God's people? How do you think they assisted in God's people not getting too proud? What do you think about the possibility of God sparing the Canaanites in order to be gracious to them so they could believe on Him for salvation?

Dear Parents,

It is an interesting fact of the Bible that though primarily the firstborn son is the most blessed, there are times when God specifically provides greater blessing for the younger. As parents, we can learn by this observation that just because it seems best for one of our children to receive a specific blessing, it is God who ultimately determines the blessing our child receives.

God's Blessing to All Generations

Read Joshua 17:1-6

✎ Observations & Questions You Have from the Passage

_____

_____

_____

_____

_____

_____

_____

_____

_____

_____

Knowing for Yourself

Manasseh was Joseph's _____ son.

Manasseh had a son named _____ .

Why was Manasseh allotted Gilead and Bashan?

- ☐ Because they liked the territory.
- ☐ Because they were men of war.

They allotted other land to the people group of Manasseh according to the _____ children of Manasseh.

Zelophehad, the great grandson of Manasseh, had no sons and only daughters. How many daughters did he have? _____

The daughters of Zelophehad came to _____ the priest, and _____ , and before _____ .

...

Family Project Idea

Begin and keep a prayer journal. Identify specific things you find in God's Word that are commanded to be given to you. Then, ask God to give you those things. Record the promised provision. Begin and continue to ask God for the promised provision. When the provision has been granted, record the date and the event. Review the journal regularly.

...

Why did the daughters of Zelophehad ask the leaders for an allotment of land to be given?

- ☐ The Lord had commanded to give them an inheritance.
- ☐ They wanted to be like the men.

The Tribe of Manasseh was given land on the east and the west side of the Jordan. (True/False)

"Prayer is the meeting of words – my words of need and God's Word of Promised Provision. "

~Anne Gurley

🖋 Thoughts and Observations for Victorious Living

† Men and women of God should keep their word and the Word of God, even though it goes against culture and tradition.

† We should be at liberty to ask God for what we need and desire.

FOR DISCUSSION

Discuss Matthew 7:7-11. How did the daughters of Zelophehad follow this principle with the leaders? How can you follow this principle in your life? Is there anything you need to start, stop, or change to make this instruction useful to you?

Dear Parents,

It is interesting that Joshua did not rally all the troops to help the people of Ephraim to occupy the land they had been given. Though they asked Joshua for assistance, he refused. Instead, he encouraged them by reminding them of the resources they had to accomplish their request. There are times we should not "do" for our children. Instead, we should encourage our children and remind them they have the necessary resources to be successful.

Work Must Be Done

Read Joshua 17:7-18

✏️ Observations & Questions You Have from the Passage

_____

_____

_____

_____

_____

_____

_____

_____

_____

_____

Knowing for Yourself

Manasseh went from Asher to _____ .

Manasseh had the land of _____ , but the border of this land belonged to the children of _____ .

What was the river at the south of the land of Manasseh? _____

FIND IT: Use a Bible atlas or online search to locate the cities discussed in Joshua 17. See the vast area given to the family of Manasseh and the land given to the family of Ephraim. Take the time to locate at least five cities mentioned in Joshua 17 on the map.

Ephraim and Manasseh met together in _____ on the north and _____ on the east.

Manasseh could not drive out the inhabitants of certain cities. What was the name of the people group they could not drive out? _____

As the children of Israel got stronger, they put the _____ to tribute (forced labor) but did not utterly drive them out.

...

The children of Joseph spoke to Joshua, saying:

☐ "We are small, you have given us too much land."
☐ "We are great, you did not give us enough land."

...

Joshua told them if Ephraim was too narrow, they should clear land for themselves of the _____ , and of the giants.

The children of Joseph were concerned because the people who lived in the hill country had _____ of iron.

What three things did Joshua tell the house of Joseph?

    †   Thou are a great _____ .

    †   Thou has great _____ .

    †   Thou shall have more than one _____ .

What did Joshua want the house of Joseph to do?

    †   Take the _____ .

    †   Cut down the _____ .

    †   Drive out the _____ .

...

Thoughts and Observations for Victorious Living

    †   Joshua passed down the Word of the Lord to the children of Joseph: "Be strong and of good courage, be thou not dismayed for the Lord thy God is with thee wherever you go."

    †   There is warning against "wanting more given to you" when you already have it and just need to work a little to utilize what you already have.

FOR DISCUSSION

Discuss Joel 3:9-11. How does the right self-talk help you in working for the use of the provision that has been provided? Is there anything you've been given that needs a little work for you to use it? How can you begin thinking rightly about it?

Dear Parents,

When your child is slow to receive the blessings of God for themselves, provide more detailed instruction. Joshua gave them the steps necessary to receive the possession. When your child doesn't grasp a truth of God, break it into smaller, more detailed parts, and guide them to "get it". Example: Take John 3:16 in parts – God's love, The World, Jesus, Believing, Death, Life. Talk about each part individually, then begin putting a few parts together, until they can grasp the whole truth of John 3:16.

Day Thirty-Four

Encouraged to Possess

Read Joshua 18:1-10

✎ Observations & Questions You Have from the Passage

_____

_____

_____

_____

_____

_____

_____

_____

_____

Knowing for Yourself

What city did the whole congregation join together? _____

How many tribes hadn't received an inheritance of land? _____

What did Joshua ask the children of Israel? "How long are you _____ to go to possess the land, which the Lord God of your fathers hath given you?"

Joshua asked for _____ men from each tribe. They were to go to _____ the land. Then they would return and report to _____ .

They would cast _____ to determine which tribes would get each portion of the land they divided out.

 INTERESTING FACT

A possession is something you acquire. The owner takes dominion over the thing possessed. Joshua was encouraging the children of Israel to move into the territories that were available for them to possess. God desires us to live in the blessing of His provision. He wants us to take possession of it.

Which tribe wouldn't get a lot of land? _____ Why?

_____

...

Where did the men write about the land they were surveying to determine the seven parts into which it would be divided?

_____

_____

_____

Who did the men return to?

_____

Who did Joshua cast lots before?

_____

Family Project Idea

Do this the next time you have a meal. Make the plates. Write everyone's name on individual pieces of paper. Place all the names in a hat. Choose a plate. Draw out a name to receive the plate. Talk about how this method of distribution feels.

Joshua divided the land to the children of Israel according to their

_____ .

 FIND IT: Proverbs 16:33 Explain how God ultimately makes the decision. How does this affect what you think about decision making?

✎ Thoughts and Observations for Victorious Living

† We should stay near the presence of the Lord when we are preparing to make decisions.

† All decisions of life should be made in the presence of the Lord.

 FOR DISCUSSION

Discuss Matthew 9:27-30. Jesus said the men were healed because of their faith. Their confidence in God's ability caused them to come to Jesus to be healed. They acted to take possession of their healing. How does this story relate to the children of Israel? Joshua made the children of Israel aware their land was waiting. How did the children of Israel act by faith to take possession of their land? Are there circumstances in your life in which God has given you something to possess and you haven't reached out to investigate, act upon it, and take it with confidence in God's provision?

Dear Parents,

Encourage your child to serve by your example of service. Joshua served faithfully as leader to the children of Israel. He went out to battle. He led by example. Show you are a servant by your acts of service to your family, your church, your community, and your world. Let the words of Jesus be your motto: "I am among you as one who serves."

Given the Land Among

Read Joshua 18:11-28

✎ Observations & Questions You Have from the Passage

_____

_____

_____

_____

_____

_____

_____

_____

_____

Knowing for Yourself

What two tribes was the land of Benjamin between? _____ and _____ .

The northern border was what city?_____ What river? _____

What wilderness was part of the land of Benjamin? _____

INTERESTING FACT

Benjamin is the youngest of all the brothers. The territory assigned to Benjamin was positioned between that of Judah and Joseph, two very important tribes. Jesus explained in Luke 22:24-27 how we should define greatness. Jesus' definition of greatness is measured by the act of serving others. Do you serve? Are you great?

What was the border of Benjamin on the east side? _____

How many cities with their villages did the children of Benjamin inherit according to their families? _____

Family Project Idea

Research some service projects you and your family could participate in. Decide which project would be most suitable for the knowledge, skills, and abilities of your family. Set a date to help. Gather the resources needed. Work in that service project as if working for the Lord. (Colossians 3:23-24)

✎ Thoughts and Observations for Victorious Living

†   God gives us allotment among and between others. However, what God gives us is ours. It does not belong to others, even though they live close by.

FOR DISCUSSION

Discuss John 13:1-17. Jesus was among His brothers. What was different about Jesus? What did His actions show? What example was Jesus giving with His actions? Was this a one-time occurrence? How should we use Jesus' example as a guide for our life? What was Jesus' attitude in serving? What should our attitude be in serving? How can we begin serving today as a way of life?

A WORD ABOUT SERVICE

Greatness is determined by humility in God's kingdom. Humility has been described as **not thinking less of yourself, but thinking of yourself less**. Service is more about a mindset than actions performed. Philippians 2 provides an excellent way to think about service. Three steps are involved in service, and Jesus Christ displayed each of these.

It is not about what you "do for God." Jesus taught in Matthew 7:22 that many would think their wonderful acts of service would get them a spot in heaven. However, Jesus said they would be turned away. Service is not great and wonderful acts. Service is a state of mind.

This mindset begins with emptying oneself. While recognizing you have great value and worth, you willingly lay all that aside to be of help to someone else. You in no way deny your value, but instead choose not to exercise it for your own advantage. Jesus displayed this perfectly. He understood Himself to be the Son of God. He knew God was His Father. He had a perfect union with God and knew the Father would do anything He asked of Him. He did not use that for His own advantage, but He emptied Himself of that privilege.

Next, service is determining to represent yourself as a servant to everyone. You think of yourself as someone *hired to work in another's household*. You are willing to do the little tasks to ensure the lives of others run successfully. Doing what needs to be done to get the job done is a motto for service. Jesus' popular example of washing the disciples' feet (John 13) was doing something for His disciples that needed to be done. He saw something that needed doing, and He did it. Service is displayed in this way.

Finally, service for others is a deep desire to take the other person's place to the greatest extent possible. Paul had a service mentality in Romans 9:3, when he desired that he could be cursed so that others could be saved. Though that was not possible, Paul had a state of mind that would have acted upon that desire if given the opportunity. Jesus had the ultimate servant's mindset for His desire to die in our place. Jesus not only had the willingness to take another's place, He did it. Jesus' death on the cross is the ultimate example of service.

Service is a mindset of humility. Let us serve by thinking of ourselves less.

NOTES

Dear Parents,

Sharing should be a way of life for a Christian. This example of the inheritance of Judah being too much for them is a way to explain to your child the importance of sharing. Talking to them about how having too much of something could be a hurtful, bad thing for them. If they share, then everyone has something and it is not too much for any one group to take care of. Discuss with your child about how to know if they have too much of something and should share.

More Than Enough

Read Joshua 19:1-16

✎ Observations & Questions You Have from the Passage

_____

_____

_____

_____

_____

_____

_____

_____

_____

Knowing for Yourself

Who came up for the second lot? _____

How many cities and villages were given to the children of Simeon?
_____

These were taken out of the land of _____ because too much land had originally been given to them.

The third lot came for the children of _____ to be assigned their land.

How many cities with their villages are part of Zebulun? _____

...

 INTERESTING FACT

Jesus' ministry began in the land of Zebulun (Matthew 5:15). It was prophesied in Isaiah 9:1-2 that the Messiah would come out of the land of Zebulun. The people of Zebulun who were in darkness would see a great light. Jesus began preaching, teaching, and calling people to repentance in the land of Zebulun.

...

✎ Thoughts and Observations for Victorious Living

† God uses what His own people have to provide blessing and help to others in His kingdom.

† God's provision may seem small. God can use small things to do great things and display His glory.

FOR DISCUSSION

Discuss the word repentance as found in Matthew 5:17 and 2 Peter 3:9. What does the word repentance mean? How do people repent? Why is repentance described as those in darkness seeing a great light? Why is repentance necessary in light of the kingdom of heaven?

Discuss 1 Kings 17:1-16. How do you share when you do not even have enough for yourself? What happened in this story with the woman who shared to help a man of God? Though the woman did not have an abundance, how did God provide for her because she shared? What do you think would have happened if she had not been willing to share?

Dear Parents,

Does your home have a reputation? If the walls of your house could speak, what would be said about the happenings among your family? Would the account be pleasing or disturbing? Take some time to reflect on these questions and determine if there are any improvements to consider.

Places with Happenings

Read Joshua 19:17-31

📝 Observations & Questions You Have from the Passage

_____

_____

_____

_____

_____

_____

_____

_____

_____

_____

Knowing for Yourself

Issachar was the _____ lot that came up.

How many cities with their villages went to the tribe of Issachar?
_____

The fifth lot came out for the tribe of the children of _____ .

Tyre was known as the "_____" city.

How many cities with their villages were given to the children of Asher? _____

 INTERESTING FACT

The Valley of Jezreel is in the land of Issachar. Many things have happened in Jezreel. Some are as follows:

† Jezebel (King Ahab's wife) was thrown down to her death. (2 Kings 9:30-35)

† Naboth refused to sell his vineyard and was murdered. (1 Kings 21:1-23)

† The Midianites and Amalekites were defeated by the Israelites. (Judges 6–8)

† King Saul and his sons were defeated by the Philistines and died. (1 Samuel 31)

...

Family Project Idea

Look up the Scripture passages and record events that occurred in the city of Tyre. 2 Samuel 5:11; 1 Kings 5:1–14; 9:11; 2 Chronicles 2:3; Ezekiel 28:1–19; Zechariah 9:2–4; Matthew 15:21–28; Acts 21:2–4

How does seeing some of the events that took place and the culture help you?

✏️ Thoughts and Observations for Victorious Living

† Everyone has their place and their possession in the presence of God.

FOR DISCUSSION

Discuss Psalm 139 with a focus on verses 23-24. Many events and activities happened in cities belonging to the land of Zebulun and the land of Issachar. Some of these events were good and some of them were bad. How does it make you feel to know God sees everything that you've ever done? Verses 23 and 24 explain how we can pray to God for searching and leading in righteousness. If the cities in Zebulun and Issachar had prayed this prayer, how might the events been different?

Dear Parents,

The day by day living in your family may seem long, tedious, and never-ending. It has been said, the only constant thing is change. So if you are in a hard season of life, if despair and despondency crowd in, know this too shall pass. There is a time and season for everything. Your season of "hard" will soon come to an end.

Respect Your Leaders

Read Joshua 19:32-51

✎ Observations & Questions You Have from the Passage

_____

_____

_____

_____

_____

_____

_____

_____

Knowing for Yourself

Which tribe was the sixth to be given land? _____

How many cities with their villages were given to the tribe of Naphtali?

_____

Bible Memorization Challenge

Proverbs 4:1-8

What was the seventh tribe to be allotted land? _____

INTERESTING FACT

Though the land of Zebulun and the land of Naphtali were distributed at different times, they bordered one another. The land of Naphtali was joined with the land of Zebulun, where Jesus began His ministry and the place mentioned in Isaiah as the place the people who sat in darkness would see a great light. Matthew 5:15; Isaiah 9:1-2

The coast of Dan was too (large/small). What did they do because of this? _____

Who did all the tribes give an inheritance to? _____

What was the name of the city Joshua built and lived in? _____

_____

Who did all the dividing? _____, _____, and

_____ .

Where were they when they were dividing the land? _____ at the Tent of Meeting.

Family Project Idea

Choose a leader or group of leaders who have helped you in life. Decide what you have that you can give them. Make sure it is something they need or could use. Give them the gift at a special service or on a special occasion. Make sure to demonstrate your appreciation for their leadership in your life. Be specific about ways they have served you, and things they've done that have helped you in life.

Thoughts and Observations for Victorious Living

† Everything will eventually come to an end.

† We as followers should take care of our leaders and provide for them.

FOR DISCUSSION

Discuss Exodus 33:7-11. What was the Tent of Meeting? What happened at the Tent of Meeting? What was Joshua's experience over the years at the Tent of Meeting? Why do you think it was important for the division of the land to be done at the Tent of Meeting? How is the Tent of Meeting similar to the presence of God and prayer today? What conclusions can you draw about making decisions for your life?

Dear Parents,

God had planned for refuge cities the whole time. However, He waited until the distribution of land was complete before initiating this new task. It is important to not overload your child with tasks. God remembered they could only do one thing at the time. It is important to ensure your children give their full attention to one task before placing on them a new task. Do not allow the word "concentration" to be removed from your child's dictionary. Encourage them to focus on the task before moving on to another task. Lead by example and demonstrate the benefits of focus.

Setting Up Refuge Cities

Read Joshua 20:1-9

✐ Observations & Questions You Have from the Passage

_____

_____

_____

_____

_____

_____

_____

Knowing for Yourself

Who initiated setting up the cities of refuge? _____

Who was Joshua supposed to talk to about setting up the cities?

_____

Who could go to the city?

☐ Someone who had hated a person for a long time and killed them.

☐ Someone who had not hated a person and an accident occurred that killed the person.

When the person fled to the city, they would have to talk to the _____ of the city before they could enter.

If the person who had been injured or someone on that person's behalf come after the person fleeing to the city, the city would deliver the person seeking refuge to the person who was pursing him. (True/False)

...

How long would he stay in the city of refuge?

†   Until he had been _____

    OR

†   Until the high priest _____

...

Match the name of the city with the tribe the city was located in.

<table>
<tr><td>Kedesh</td><td>Reuben</td></tr>
<tr><td>Shechem</td><td>Naphtali</td></tr>
<tr><td>Kirjatharba/Hebron</td><td>Gad</td></tr>
<tr><td>Bezer</td><td>Manasseh</td></tr>
<tr><td>Ramoth</td><td>Ephraim</td></tr>
<tr><td>Golan</td><td>Judah</td></tr>
</table>

These cities were appointed for both the children of Israel and others who lived with them. (True/False)

The cities of refuge allowed a person to _____ the hand of someone who was trying to get him back for a crime he may have done by accident.

Family Project Idea

Play a game of Refuge. Establish a place to be a Refuge City. Assign the following participants: Priest, Elder, Guilty Person, Refuge Townspeople, Victim, Victim's Friends, Hometown People.

Act out a few scenarios where the Guilty Person pretends to hurt someone and flees to the Refuge City. The Elders interview him before letting him in. The Hometown People come after him. Allow the game to be an experience of what it may have been like to have fled to a Refuge City. Be sure to play until the Guilty can get released from the Refuge City.

✎ Thoughts and Observations for Victorious Living

† God provides a way of escape when we "mess up" without meaning to. He provides a "refuge" and allows us protection from others.

Dear Parents,

Pastors are your leaders today. What are you doing as a family to support your pastor? Are you teaching your children to not only listen to your pastor, but to provide encouraging feedback and support to your pastor? Does your family give of what you've been given to help support your pastor's family? If so, keep up your God-given duty. If not, decide one thing you can do right away for your pastor.

Day Forty

God Provides for the Priests

Read Joshua 21:1-12

✎ **Observations & Questions You Have from the Passage**

_____

_____

_____

_____

_____

_____

_____

_____

_____

_____

_____

_____

_____

Knowing for Yourself

The heads of the fathers of the tribe of _____ came before Joshua, Eleazar the priest, and the heads of the fathers of the tribes of the children of Israel.

They met in the land of _____ .

The Levite leaders claimed _____ had commanded the Levites to be given cities to dwell in and keep their cattle.

Who commanded that the Levites be given cities to dwell in and keep their cattle? _____

Judah, Simeon, and Benjamin gave _____ cities.

INTERESTING FACT

Acts 2:44-45 describes a similar distribution as was seen in Joshua 21. The distribution in Acts was to anyone in the assembly that had need. Everyone pooled all their resources together. They truly lived as one family. They trusted one another. They confided in one another. They lived together in peace. Everyone looked out for one another and shared all they had to meet all needs.

Ephraim, Dan, and the half tribe of Manasseh gave _____ cities.

Issachar, Asher, and Naphtali gave _____ cities.

Reuben, Gad, and Zebulun gave _____ cities.

How were the cities distributed to the Levites? _____

...

Which of the Levitical families received the first distribution of the land? _____

Who also shared Hebron with Aaron? _____

✎ Thoughts and Observations for Victorious Living

† God provides for His servants and people who do the work of the Kingdom.

† God allows those to whom He has given wealth and possession to share with those who have need.

FOR DISCUSSION

Discuss the reason the Levites did not initially have a territory of land given to them. However, now they are receiving land from each tribe. Could it have anything to do with God wanting His priests to be accessible to the people? What is the value of the allotment of land?

A WORD ABOUT REFUGE

Psalm 91 is a song of security for the believer. It affirms whoever seeks shelter in the Lord from danger will truly find it. This decision to make the Lord your trust and security is an intentional determination.

There are many benefits to seeking shelter in God. There is help for deadly epidemic or plague. The truth of God preserves you from the enemy, who shoots darts intended to wound. God is near to you so much you can feel His presence surrounding you and protecting you. Though you see others falling, you are strong and secure because you are trusting in God.

Time must be spent under the shelter of God's refuge for the benefit to really be seen. Just as the person seeking refuge had to remain in the refuge city, we must remain in the refuge of God. John 15 uses the word "abide." We must remain in God's Word and God's Word in us. We cannot rush in and out of God's presence. We must sit and stay a while. The longer we remain, the more we have opportunity to experience the nearness of God. Then, we trust Him more and more.

A feature of refuge is prayer. When the people seeking refuge came to the city, they "prayed" to the elders, pleading their case for why they should be allowed in to receive shelter. When we seek refuge in God, we call upon Him. We plead our case for why He should give us protection. The reason that works every time for God to protect us and help us is because we know His name. That means we know His reputation to take care of the weak, needy, and afflicted. We recognize we are in need and He is the only one who can help. God answers and provides us shelter because we fix our affection on Him.

The refuge cities were set up to protect the guilty from the victim. Just as the guilty ran for refuge to the refuge city, we run for refuge to God. We are the guilty and He is our protector. We know His reputation of safe, secure help. Therefore, we call upon Him. He hears us and provides the protection we seek.

READ PSALM 91 & MAKE GOD YOUR REFUGE TODAY.

NOTES

_____

_____

_____

_____

_____

_____

_____

_____

_____

_____

_____

Dear Parents,

Have you established a "safe place" in your home?
Is there a place where open and honest discussions
can be held? Where things can be openly expressed
by your child without their fearing your wrath or
condemnation? It is important for you to establish
a "safe plac" for your child to have opportunity to
tell of their struggles, fears, and hardships.

The Cities Assigned

Read Joshua 21:13-33

✎ **Observations & Questions You Have from the Passage**

_____

_____

_____

_____

_____

_____

_____

_____

_____

_____

Knowing for Yourself

How many cities did they give to Aaron the priest? _____

What was the name of the city given to Aaron? _____

How many cities to dwell in were given to the family of Aaron?

_____

The people of Ephraim gave the cities they donated to the children of _____ .

What city was given to Kohath? _____

 FIND IT: Locate a map of the Levite cities. Notice how they are scattered. Check a few verses to identify the city is located in the territory of land as stated in Joshua 21.

...

How many cities to dwell in were given to the family of Kohath? _____

The family of the children of Gershon received two cities of refuge. What were the names of the cities? _____

 INTERESTING FACT

The Levites had to be satisfied with what they were given. As New Testament believers, we also have to be satisfied. Another word for satisfied is content. 1 Timothy 6:6-7 remind us that having contentment and godliness is of much advantage. The reason for this is because we brought nothing into this world and we will take nothing with us when we leave. Think about this fact as you make daily decisions.

✐ Thoughts and Observations for Victorious Living

† God owns everything and had provided cities for the children of Israel, so it was God's property they were giving to the families of the high priests.

FOR DISCUSSION

Discuss Psalm 50:10. How does this Scripture illustrate that God owns everything? In what ways does God have "permission" to give land and distribute land? Did the tribes that gave the Levites the cities to dwell in have a choice to give to the Levites?

Dear Parents,

The day-to-day grind of life can discourage us from seeing the fruit of our labor. Keep planting the seeds you want to see produced in your children. The more you plant and water, the more God is able to do abundantly above all you could ask, think, hope, or imagine. Joshua in his 95 years of dealing with the children of Israel no doubt felt discouraged at times. But he kept persisting and as everything God commanded is taking place, he sees the fruit of his labor.

God Accomplishes All He Intended

Read Joshua 21:34-45

✎ Observations & Questions You Have from the Passage

_____

_____

_____

_____

_____

_____

_____

Knowing for Yourself

What was the name of the fourth family of the tribe of Levi?

_____

How many cities did the family of Merari receive? _____

How many cities did the Levites possess out of all the land of the children of Israel? _____

Who gave the children of Israel the land to possess? _____

The Lord gave them _____ all around from their enemies.

The Lord had told the forefathers He would NOT give them rest. (True/False)

Enemies stood against the children of Israel on every side. (True/False)

...

Every enemy was defeated and delivered into the hands of the children of Israel. (True/False)

Everything God said would happen, happened. (True/False)

God withheld every good thing from the children of Israel. (True/False)

...

Family Project Idea

Research the lineage of Levi. Create a family tree that represents each of the ancestors of Levi.

...

✏ Thoughts and Observations for Victorious Living

  † God is faithful. He keeps His Word.

  † God gives victory over our enemies and things that come against us.

  † Nothing can stand in victory over the Lord God.

FOR DISCUSSION

Discuss Malachi 3:10. God promised to bless when His people gave a tenth of all their possessions to Him. When the Levites received a distribution of land, that was a way the tribes were giving back to the Lord a portion of what they had been given. What principle can you establish for yourself? How can you establish a practical way to implement this principle in your life?

Dear Parents,

take the time to regularly call
your children and commend them
for their hearing, keeping, and
doing what you instructed them.

| Day Forty-three | **Go Home and Don't Forget**
Read Joshua 22:1-10 |

✎ Observations & Questions You Have from the Passage

_____

_____

_____

_____

_____

_____

Knowing for Yourself

Joshua called which three tribes in order to speak to them?

_____

_____

_____

Joshua commended the people for the following:

† Keeping all that _____ the servant of the Lord commanded.

† Obeying all that _____ had commanded.

† Not leaving their _____ .

† Kept doing all that _____ had commanded.

Joshua told the people because the Lord had given _____ to everyone, they could return home.

What did Joshua tell them to do once they returned home?

† Be _____ to do all the commandment of the law.

† _____ the Lord their God.

† _____ in all the Lord's ways.

† _____ the Lord's commandments.

† _____ the Lord with all their _____ and _____ .

...

Family Project Idea

Create a list of reminders that can be shared with family members as they leave the house to spend the night with a friend or when going away to college. Use the reminders Joshua gave the tribes going back on the east side of the Jordan as a guide. Make it look nice and place it close by the door.

...

Where did the men of Reuben, Gad, and the half tribe of Manasseh go? _____

What separated the people in the half tribe of Manasseh?

_____

Joshua sent them home with much riches, which consisted of:

† _____

† _____

† _____

† _____

Joshua told them to _____ what they had been given with their brothers.

What did the people do when they got back home? _____ .

...

Thoughts and Observations for Victorious Living

† Obedience is repaid with rest and blessing.

† God provides enough for us to be able to share with others.

† The Lord and His ways should be our primary focus.

...

FOR DISCUSSION

Discuss Psalm 78:1-9. How had Joshua done what this passage says? How are your passing on God's ways to the next generation?

Dear Parents,

Inquire before judging is an important motto for any leader. Your children may have the appearance of doing something inappropriate. However, before accusing them of misbehavior, inquire of their motivation. Provide correction when necessary. Discourage any appearance of evil. Most importantly, respect your child enough to give them a hearing. Finally, guide them into all truth. If your child knows they have been fully heard, they likely will fully hear you.

What Are You Doing?

Read Joshua 22:11-20

✎ Observations & Questions You Have from the Passage

_____

_____

_____

_____

_____

_____

_____

Knowing for Yourself

When the children of Israel heard about the altar, they gathered at Shiloh to make _____ against Reuben, Gad, and the half tribe of Manasseh.

The people sent _____ the priests and _____ leaders (one from each of the tribes).

Eleazar and the leaders spoke for the whole _____ .
They thought the men building the altar were _____ against the Lord.

The leaders thought God would be _____ and punish the whole people because of the altar that had been built.

The spokespeople told Reuben, Gad, and the half tribe of Manasseh if their land was not clean, they should move back to the other side of the Jordan. (True/False)

Phinehas and the leaders reminded the people of another person who sinned and caused a lot of people to die. What was that person's name? _____

...

Bible Memorization Challenge

Proverbs 13:20 † 1 Corinthians 15:33

...

✎ Thoughts and Observations for Victorious Living

†   We should recognize our kinship with others. When we see they may be going astray, go visit them and talk openly with them.

†   Protecting God's name and reverencing Him should be primary in our life.

†   When we sin, it affects others.

FOR DISCUSSION

Discuss Romans 16:17-18. What are these verses saying? How did the leaders follow this teaching when confronting the tribes of Gad, Reuben, and the half tribe of Manasseh? What do you notice about their accusations? Did the leaders jump to conclusions or talk about the matter? How can you talk to someone who says they are a Christian but appears to be doing something contrary to the Bible? Role play a scenario or scenarios for practice.

Dear Parents,

What are you doing today to keep your children walking in the ways of the Lord in the future? This passage is a great example of the needed forethought of parents. Begin today thinking about what kind of future you want your children to have with God and implement strategies to keep them victorious in the Lord.

| Day Forty-Five | **Conflict Resolved** |
| | Read Joshua 22:21-34 |

✐ Observations & Questions You Have from the Passage

_____

_____

_____

_____

_____

_____

_____

_____

Knowing for Yourself

What did the children of Reuben, Gad, and the half tribe of Manasseh answer to Phinehas and the others who had come to them?

†   God knows why we built this altar, let _____ know also.

†   If we built an altar to turn away from God, you can _____ us.

†   If we built this altar to turn from following the Lord, may _____ come against us.

† In the future, your children may say to our children, you have no part in _____ and make our children stop serving the Lord.

† We built this altar as a _____ between us on the east side and you on the west side of the Jordan that we would be servants of your God and ours.

† The altar would be a _____ to all that we follow the Lord God of Israel even though we are on a different side of the Jordan.

...

When Phinehas and the leaders heard what Reuben and the half tribe of Manasseh had answered, they were _____ .

Why had Phinehas and the leaders decided God was with them?

_____

...

When Phinehas and the men returned to the children of Israel and explained the situation, how did they respond? _____

_____

What was the name of the altar that had been built? _____

...

✐ Thoughts and Observations for Victorious Living

† Think ahead for those who will come behind you and do all you can to protect them from falling away from the Lord.

† Hear all reasons before making war.

† God is with us when we do not trespass against Him.

FOR DISCUSSION

Discuss Proverbs 18:30. How is this verse of wisdom relevant to the potential disagreement in Joshua 22? What was avoided because the matter was heard? When you have a potential disagreement with someone, how would this verse be helpful? How does this verse apply in the following relationship: parent/child; teacher/student; friend/friend; neighbor/neighbor? What are some ways you can practice this verse in your life?

A WORD ABOUT WORSHIP

Worship is **bowing the knee**. It is a lowering of oneself in the presence of someone greater. Jesus' famous encounter with the woman at the well in John 4 speaks to the primary relationship of people to God. Jesus said God is looking for people who will *bow the knee* to Him in spirit and in truth.

The woman at the well was concerned with the place people worship. Jesus told her not to be concerned with the place. He told her the knowledge of who the knee was bowed to was of more importance than the place the knee was bowed.

Worship is a giving of worth. When we worship, we pin value on the one to whom we are lowering ourselves. God desires all men to bow their knee to Him in spirit and in truth. It is not that we make up things to praise the Lord for in worship. Instead, we confidently identify and declare the things God is or does that make Him so great.

Psalm 95 is an example of worship. The children of Israel, entering the promised land, received rest from war and ability to enjoy the land. They took the time to bow the knee to God by doing the following:

   † Singing to God, for He is the foundation of their deliverance.

   † Praising God with the giving of thanks for all His provision.

   † Knowing the Lord is the God above all gods.

   † Acknowledging God has made the whole world and possesses everything in His hands.

   † Kneeling before the God who made them.

These examples represent the proper way to worship God in spirit and in truth. The knowledge of who God is and what He has done enables us to know who we worship. We are bowing down to the one we "know." We acknowledge who He is and what He has done. The expression of what we know God to be and who God is allows us to worship in spirit and in truth.

NOTES

_____

_____

_____

_____

_____

_____

_____

_____

_____

_____

_____

_____

_____

Dear Parents,

Notice how Joshua always directed the people to
look to God. As parents, we should always direct our
children to look to God. We should remind them of all
God has done for them in their personal history and
in biblical history. We should also remind our children
God is "fighting" for them. This regular encouragement
will be beneficial to your children on many levels.

Keep Doing What You've Been Doing

Read Joshua 23:1-8

📝 Observations & Questions You Have from the Passage

_____

_____

_____

_____

_____

_____

_____

Knowing for Yourself

Right after the Lord had given rest to the land, Joshua recognized he was old. (True/False)

Joshua called all Israel, which included the following:

✝ _____

✝ _____

✝ _____

✝ _____

What did Joshua tell them?

    ✝   I am _____ .

    ✝   You have seen all that the Lord did to these nations because

        _____ .

    ✝   The Lord God _____ for you.

    ✝   Joshua had divided the _____ to the
        great sea westward.

...

What would God do with the people of the nations that still remained in the land the children of Israel possessed? _____

How could the children of Israel be sure they would have complete possession of the land? _____

...

Because of all God had done for them:

    ✝   Fought for them.

    ✝   Gave them land.

    ✝   Drove out the people before them.

What was to be their response?

    ✝   Be very _____ to keep and to do all
        that is written in The Book of the Law.

    ✝   Do not _____ to the right or the left.

    ✝   Do not _____ the gods of the nations
        or call on them in anyway.

    ✝   _____ to the Lord your God.

INTERESTING FACT

Moses had first told Joshua to be strong and very courageous. Now, half of a century later, Joshua is encouraging the generation after him to be strong and very courageous. Joshua had promoted this "self-talk" within himself. He wanted those coming after him to have the same encouragement.

Thoughts and Observations for Victorious Living

†   We have victory because God fights for us.

†   The response to God because of His help and provision to us should be a response of strong courage to obey, keep on keeping on, and stay close to God.

FOR DISCUSSION

Discuss the language "cleave," "cling," "hold-fast" found in Joshua 23:8. What does this language mean? What do you have to do to act upon this command? What are some specific habits in your daily living you could establish (or keep doing) to ensure you stay close to God? Do you need accountability to do this?

Dear Parents,

The most beneficial instruction you can give your child is to love God. Their love of God will be the determining factor of their well-being both now and for all eternity. Do not neglect this most basic and necessary of duties.

Stay Close to God

Read Joshua 23:9-16

✏ **Observations & Questions You Have from the Passage**

_____

_____

_____

_____

_____

_____

_____

_____

Knowing for Yourself

Who drove out the great and strong nations before the children of Israel? _____

Who was able to fight and stand up against the children of Israel?

_____

One man could chase 1,000 alone because:

- † The Lord _____ for you.
- † The Lord _____ to you.

Because of the gracious favor and provision of the Lord, the children of Israel were admonished to _____ to love the Lord your God.

What would happen if they didn't love the Lord and started serving the gods of the nations?

† God would (continue to/no longer) drive out the nations before you.

† The nations would be (joy/snares and traps) to you.

† The nations would be (smooth and safe/rough and hurtful) to you.

† You will (live forever on/perish from) the earth.

Family Project Idea

Joshua warned the people to not join together with the gods of other nations or take on their ways. Make a list of strategies your family could implement that would protect you from being influenced by people who do not follow God.

Joshua reminded the children of Israel (not one thing/a few things) had failed of all God told them that would happen.

...

Joshua told the leaders that just as all God's good provision had come upon them as God had promised, if they disobeyed and turned away from God, what would happen? _____

What would happen if the children of Israel failed to keep the covenant of the Lord their God?

  †   God would be _____ with them.

  †   They would _____ from the land.

Who gave the children of Israel the land they possessed? _____

INTERESTING FACT

God is a right judge and has the "right" to judge the wicked. He is angry at the wicked every day. (Psalm 7:11)

✏️ Thoughts and Observations for Victorious Living

  †   God fights for us and promises to provide for us.

  †   We can be sure to make God angry and cause ourselves difficulty when we don't take heed to stay close and obedient to the Lord.

FOR DISCUSSION

Discuss Jeremiah 1:12. God told Jeremiah He was "watching over His word to perform it." Did God do that in the book of Joshua? Give examples for your response.

Dear Parents,

Rehearse all God has done often with your children. Psalm 139 is a useful Scripture to help your children understand that before they were created, God had a plan for them. Joshua reminded the children of Israel that God had a plan for them that went all the way back to Abraham. Joshua retold all God had done. Retell all God has done in the life of your child.

Everything You Have Came from God

Read Joshua 24:1-13

✎ Observations & Questions You Have from the Passage

_____

_____

_____

_____

_____

_____

_____

_____

Knowing for Yourself

Where did Joshua call all the tribes, leaders, and elders of Israel?

_____

Who did they present themselves before? _____

Joshua spoke words to the people. Whose words did he speak?

_____

What were the things the Lord had
done for the people that Joshua
reminded the people of?

Family Project Idea

**Read the account of Balak
and Balaam recorded in
Numbers 22 and 23. Act out
the story as a family.**

† Their _____
had lived on the other side
of the flood (Euphrates River).

† _____ the father
of Abraham and Nachor served other gods.

† _____ took Abraham from the other side
of the Euphrates River (flood).

† God led Abraham throughout all _____ .

† God multiplied Abraham's seed and gave him

_____ .

...

Isaac had two sons, Jacob and Esau. What part of the land did God
give Esau to possess? _____

Where did Jacob and his family go down to? _____

...

God sent Moses and Aaron to bring the children of Israel out of
Egypt. What took place before the children of Israel went out?

_____

God delivered the children of Israel by way of the _____
and the Egyptians were drowned.

God _____ for Israel that they might possess their land.

Who gave the people land they did not labor for and vineyards and olive yards they did not plant? _____

...

Thoughts and Observations for Victorious Living

†   God delivers us from all our enemies.

†   We can trust God to hear and answer us when we pray.

†   God uses the possessions of others to meet our needs.

FOR DISCUSSION

Discuss Isaiah 54:17. How did this verse prove true in the book of Joshua? Have you seen any instances in your life where this has proven true? What are some ways you can begin making record of the protection of the Lord in your life?

Dear Parents,

Talk openly with your children about the benefits and consequences associated with their decision to follow the Lord. Encourage them to understand it is their decision and they will reap the consequences (good or evil) of their decision. Remind your children the decision they make to follow the Lord is a daily decision. They must continually shun evil and honor God. Make sure they are "in it for the long haul".

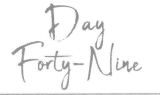

| Day Forty-Nine | **Make Your Choice**
Read Joshua 24:14-28 |

✎ Observations & Questions You Have from the Passage

_____

_____

_____

_____

_____

_____

_____

_____

Knowing for Yourself

Joshua helped the children of Israel remember all the Lord had done to rescue them out of Egypt, remove people from the land, and give them the land. Joshua gave instruction to the people in "light" of all the Lord had done for them. What was the instruction?

† _____ the Lord.

† Serve the Lord in _____ and _____ .

† Put away _____ gods.

† _____ the Lord.

Joshua gave the people a choice to serve _____ or the _____ their ancestors had served before they left Egypt.

What was Joshua's decision about whom he would serve?

_____

Family Project Idea

Compose a family covenant to serve the Lord. Make it look official. Have everyone in the family sign it. Set it in a place so it can be remembered.

What was the people's decision? _____

What was the reason they would serve the Lord?

- † God had brought them out of Egypt, performed great signs for them to see, drove out the people before them, and gave them the land.
- † God was making them serve Him. They did not have a choice.

Joshua warned the people that God is a _____ God and if they turned away, did not obey Him, and transgressed against God, He would _____ them.

Bible Memorization Challenge

Joshua 24:14-15

...

Because the people had chosen to follow the Lord, Joshua told the people they needed to:

- † Put away _____ gods.
- † _____ heart unto the Lord God of Israel.
- † Joshua made them a covenant (agreement) and set up statutes and ordinances in _____ .

Joshua wrote all the words in a _____ and set
up a great _____ .

What was the purpose of the stone? _____

Where did everyone go? _____

 Thoughts and Observations for Victorious Living

† Before we choose to serve God, we should clearly understand
all God has done for us.

† We must make a decision to serve God and act upon that
decision by removing everything that is against God and
inclining unto God.

† Setting up a remembrance of the decision made to serve
God will help in future.

† God will punish the guilty, those who do not keep His ways.

FOR DISCUSSION

Discuss the importance of making a decision
about who you will serve. Talk about how to
"stick with" the decision. Determine what happens
when a decision is "put off" or "not kept." Write out
anything that needs to be remembered from this
discussion.

Dear Parents,

Joshua lived his life in the way he wanted to be remembered when he died. He was remembered as a son of Nun and as a servant of the Lord. How do you want to be remembered when you die? Are you living toward that end today?

Joshua Dies

Read Joshua 24:29-33

✎ Observations & Questions You Have from the Passage

_____

_____

_____

_____

_____

_____

_____

Knowing for Yourself

How old was Joshua when he died? _____

What was Joshua's father's name? _____

Joshua was known as the _____ of the Lord.

Where did they bury Joshua? _____

The people served the Lord all the days of Joshua and the leaders
who lived longer than Joshua. (True/False)

Joseph had died in Egypt. When the children of Israel left Egypt, they brought his bones with them. Where did they bury Joseph's bones?

_____

Who received the land where they buried Joseph's bones?

_____

INTERESTING FACT

Genesis 50:25 records the request of Joseph to have his bones taken out of Egypt and buried in the Promised Land. It is also interesting to know Joseph died at 110 just like Joshua.

Eleazar was the son of _____ .

What happened to Eleazar? _____

Where did they bury Eleazar? _____

...

Thoughts and Observations for Victorious Living

† Human leaders die.

† Great leaders are servants.

† Knowing the works of the Lord provides greater reverence and awe of God and causes us to serve Him.

FOR DISCUSSION

Discuss Hebrews 9:27. How do you think Joshua was judged after his death? When your death comes, how will you be judged? Is there a way you can prepare ahead for the judgment of the Lord after your death? Review the parable in Matthew 25:14-30 which provides the way to judge a faithful servant.

A WORD ABOUT HEARING THE VOICE OF GOD

One of the declarations the children of Israel made to Joshua was that they would obey the voice of the Lord. How would they know the voice of the Lord in order to obey Him? How can we hear the voice of God today?

The voice of God can be heard from the words He has already spoken. The children of Israel had the law God had given to Moses. Every word in the law of Moses was given by God and was His voice. Therefore, they would know they were "hearing the voice of God" when they read the words of the Law.

Today, we can know that when we read God's Word, we are hearing the voice of God. We can be sure every word of the Bible is profitable to instruct us and teach us how to please God. (2 Timothy 3:16)

Jesus gave us further confirmation that we can hear God's voice. We know that we hear His voice when we follow Him. John 10:4 explains that those who respond to the voice of God are the ones who hear the voice of God.

If you are wondering how to hear the voice of God, first expose yourself on a regular basis to God's Word. Do what it says as diligently as possible. Change your ways to adapt to the instruction you are reading. As you conform your ways to the ways of God, you will recognize that you are following God and will know you are hearing the voice of God.

Joshua warned the children of Israel to put away all the other influences they had in their life like strange gods of the surrounding nations, friendship with the non-God people, and having close relationships with non-believers.

Hearing God's voice has not changed. Psalm 19:7-11 conveys that the voice of the Lord is best heard through the law, testimony, precepts, and commandments recorded in the Bible.

HEARING THE VOICE OF GOD OCCURS BEST WHEN WE LISTEN ONLY TO HIM AND BECOME DEAF TO OTHER INFLUENCES.

NOTES

_____

_____

_____

_____

_____

_____

_____

_____

_____

_____

_____

More Facts

Abraham – Known as the *Father of a Great Nation*, he was chosen and called by God to this task. His story begins in Genesis 12.

The Ark of the Covenant – This was a chest God instructed Moses to have built. It held replicas from the children of Israel's exodus from Egypt and wilderness journey. This was a sacred chest that had to be carried in a specific way and could only be carried by the high priests. More details can be found in Exodus 25:10-22.

The Book of the Law – These written Scriptures available at the time of Joshua likely included the tablets of stone Moses recorded after the Exodus. There may have been some historical accountings written by Moses and others. The Book of the Law consisted of God's way of doing things which was to be read, learned, and studied so that it could be obeyed in a person's daily living.

Covenant of Circumcision – This was a sign God used to display the people belonged to Him. More can be found in Genesis 17. Being part of God's people by this covenant meant they were blessed.

The Exodus – This speaks of God's call to Moses to lead the chosen people of God out of Egypt. This event included the ten plagues leading up to the crossing of the Red Sea on dry ground because of God's intervention. See Exodus 3 through 15 for further study.

Isaac – This was Abraham's son. He was a son of promise. Abraham and his wife, Sarah, were old and beyond the years of having children. Yet, God provided Isaac to Abraham. God told Abraham that it was through Isaac he would be *the Father of a Great Nation*. His story begins in Genesis 21.

Jacob – This was Isaac's son. He had a twin brother, Esau. Jacob was the second born of the twins and was not in line to get the blessing of his father. However, Esau sold Jacob his birthright and Jacob deceived his father to obtain the firstborn's blessing. Jacob fled from his brother, Esau, and worked many years for his uncle. Jacob had 12 sons. God changed Jacob's name to Israel. The names of the tribes of Israel are the names of his sons. His story begins in Genesis 25:26.

The Manna – God provided manna for the children of Israel to eat in the wilderness. This manna continued until they crossed over the Jordan and began eating the fruit of the land. See Genesis 16 and Joshua 5 for more detail.

Moses – This man began as a baby born at the time when boy children were being killed. His mother saved him from being murdered. By a sovereign series of events, Moses grew up as the son of the daughter of the Pharaoh of Egypt. However, he did not accept this high privilege. He chose rather to be known as one of God's people. He was called by God to lead the children of Israel out of Egypt. His story begins in Exodus 2.

The Passover – This was an event established on the last night before the Exodus from Egypt. Each household was responsible to kill a lamb, put the blood on the doorpost of their home, roast the lamb by fire, eat the lamb with unleavened bread and bitter herbs, and remain in the house. When the death angel came and saw the blood, he would pass over that house and the firstborn would not die. In households that did not have the blood on the doorpost, the firstborn son would die. This Passover was a regular celebration for the children of Israel as a reminder of God's salvation. This event begins in Exodus 12.

Easy Location Guide

Bible Memorization Challenges

Family Project Ideas

Have You Taken the First Step?

Before you can lead your family to victorious living, you must be sure you have taken the first step. The journey of victorious living would be impossible unless you have a relationship with God. Joshua had a relationship with God. Here's the path to a relationship with God:

† God wants you to know for sure you have a relationship with Him. (1 John 5:13)

† God has promised to have a relationship with you forever through His Son Jesus Christ. This relationship is not just for life after you die, but for your life now also. (Romans 6:23)

† There is nothing you can do to deserve God to love you or have a relationship with you. This relationship with God is totally undeserved. It is a gift of God by grace. Grace is defined as *unmerited favor*. (Ephesians 2:8,9)

† God is perfect. There is nothing in God that has any error or fault. However, you are a sinner. You were born as a sinner. No one ever had to teach you how to lie, cheat, or take something that was not yours. God never lies, cheats, or takes anything that is not His. This proves how you are a sinner and not like God. You and all of mankind come short when compared to God. No matter how hard you try, you could never measure up to the perfection and greatness of God. (Romans 3:23, Matthew 5:48)

† God does not want to leave you separated from Him, so He has bridged the gap between mankind and Himself. God is love. That means God is patient, kind, tenderhearted, and forgiving. He has loved you with a love that has always been

and will always continue. His love lasts forever. Because of God's perfection, He cannot allow anything that kills, steals, or destroys into His presence. Therefore, He must punish sin, disobedience, and the soul that sins. All the things that kill, steal, and destroy end in death. This is the great conflict. God loves you, but He must punish you because you sin. (1 John 4:8, Jeremiah 31:3, Exodus 34:7, Ezekiel 18:4)

† God sent His only Son, Jesus Christ, into the world that whoever believes on Him doesn't have to be punished because of their sin. That means when you believe on Jesus, you don't have to be punished for your own sin. Instead, God punished Jesus on your behalf. Jesus was God and came in the likeness of man. He lived among men, was perfect, and never did anything wrong. He willingly, at God's pleasure, died on a cross to take the punishment for your sin. God allowed Jesus to die in your place. God laid on Jesus all the wrong things that you have ever done or ever will do. Because Jesus took the punishment for your sin, you don't have to take that punishment. You do not have to die for your sins. Instead, Jesus died for your sins. This means when you believe on Jesus as your Savior, you have eternal life through Jesus Christ. (Isaiah 53:6, John 3:16, John 1:1, 14)

† You must put your confidence in God and believe Jesus died for your sins. You must receive Jesus as your Savior. You must recognize that God accepts you not because of the good things you've done. Instead, God accepts you because of the death of Jesus in your place. It was the death of Jesus, taking the punishment for your sin, that keeps you from having to take the punishment for your sins. That means you have eternal life through Jesus Christ. When you put your trust on Jesus Christ, you will be saved. You are saved from God's punishment of your sin. Jesus took that punishment for you. (Acts 16:31)

† It is not God's will that anyone die for their own sin. God sent Jesus into the world to rescue the world. God wants you to

believe on the Lord Jesus Christ and be saved. He wants to give you the spirit of Jesus to live inside of you to teach you how to live as a child of God. Jesus was God's only Son. Now through the death of Jesus, He is bringing many sons to God. God highly approved of His Son Jesus and wants everyone to follow Jesus' example. God wants everyone to do things like Jesus did things. (2 Peter 3:9; John 3:17-19, John 14:26; Hebrews 2:10, Galatians 3:10-14; John 15:7-9)

If you have not taken the first step, do it today. Recognize Jesus as your Savior, the one who died in your place. Receive Jesus as your Lord, the one who teaches and reminds you what to do. Turn away from everything in your life that steals, kills, and destroys. Learn what pleases God through the reading, study, and meditation of His Word. Talk to Him as friend with friend in prayerful communion. Rejoice in His payment for all the sins in your life that separated you from the perfection and greatness of God. Finally, lead your family to victorious living one day at a time.

References and Contribution Credit Page

Online References

https://www.blueletterbible.org/

https://en.wikipedia.org/wiki/Ark_of_the_Covenant

https://en.wikipedia.org/wiki/Book_of_Joshua

https://en.wikipedia.org/wiki/Ford_(crossing)

https://www.gotquestions.org/Book-of-Joshua.html

https://lifehopeandtruth.com/prophecy/12-tribes-of-israel/the-12-tribes-of-israel/

http://www.ttb.org/docs/default-source/notes-outlines/no7_joshua-judges-ruth.pdf?sfvrsn=2

https://ww2.odu.edu/~lmusselm/plant/bible/flax.php

http://jesuswalk.com

Book References

The Full Life Study Bible (1992). Grand Rapids, MI: Zondervan

Weirsbe, W. (1993). *Be Strong*. Colorado Spring, CO: David C. Cook

About the Author

Anne Gurley has a Bachelor's Degree in Middle Grades Education and is employed full time using her technical training. She has over 25 years of experience working in the local church in a variety of Children's Ministries and Women's Ministries positions. She is founder of *Life and Peace Ministries* which encourages women to find wholeness through being spiritually minded.

Anne lives in Pikeville, NC, with her husband, Jamie, and their children, Austin and Elizabeth. She loves to cook and find easy, practical recipes on Pinterest.

Made in the USA
Columbia, SC
23 December 2021

52629723R00135